THE BEST YOU CAN BE!

A rallying call to great accomplishments

KELIAS PHIRI

Cover design by Newton Mwale

ISBN: 978-99882-70-745-9

Typesetting by Kelias Phiri

Edited by Elder Fred Sichilongo

Have faith and hope and your other side written by Shadreck George Mwanza

Published by Oracles Publishers

Email: keliasphiri@gmail.com
Facebook: Kelias Phiri
Phone No: +260 955 795 961

DEDICATION

I dedicate this book to the beautiful lady envisioned to be my future bride and the children that our marriage will procreate.

I wish to also dedicate the book to my parents for ensuring that I get good education. Lastly to all my friends and all those who are visionaries in life.

TABLE OF CONTENTS

<u>ACKNOWLEDGMENT</u>

From the outset, I would like to thank the Almighty God from the bottom of my heart for His guidance through all the stages of writing and completion this book. During the journey, I encountered diverse stumbling blocks which I ultimately did overcome only because of God's grace.

In addition, I would like to express my profound gratitude to all those who in one way or another, rendered their support towards the realization of this book project. Consequently, I would like to acknowledge the valuable contributions of the following people: Mr. Shadreck George Mwanza, Mr. Kelvin Lungu, Mr. Musa George Mwanza, Mr. Teddyson Phiri, Mr. Obby Mundia, Mr. Vincent Mwanza, Ms.Edna Njovu, Ms. Esther Mwansa, Mr. Newton Mwale and Elder Fred Sichilongo.

DEAR READER,

My earnest prayer is that you may live a fulfilled life as you hopefully draw inspiration from the contents of this book. The word of God has been my prime inspiration in all my pursuits. I have also been greatly motivated by a number of men and women who against all odds have made significant strides in this life irrespective of their backgrounds.

If you meticulously practice the principles and advice contained in this book, your life will never be the same again. I can assertively guarantee you that this book will be of great help in your life's journey. In view of that, I entreat you to seek after things which are pure, lovely and of good report.

<u>FOREWORD</u>

In Zambia, there has been a significant swing towards Christianity during the past few decades. Today approximately two thirds of the Zambian population comprise Christians compared to a paltry one third documented in the 1960s. Believers in Jesus Christ have been called upon, and rightly so, to base their hope and faith in Him. Just like people of divergent faiths, Christians do from time to time undergo all potential setbacks in their walk with God. When trials and temptations arise, it is important that unwavering trust in the Son of God is upheld. But to uphold steadfast trust, we should totally yield our wills to Christ and let Him take full control of our lives.

A story is told of an American athlete by the name of Owen who while in high school had a burning desire to become an accomplished sportsman. One day he asked his coach what it would take for him to achieve his ambition. His coach highlighted four things: **_determination, dedication, discipline and attitude_**. Owen took advantage of that information and accepted the challenge. Buoyed by these inspiring words from the coach; Owen went on to win four gold medals at the 1926 Olympics. Besides that, he had set a world record which remained unbroken for twenty-two years.

This book is certainly a source of optimism, hope and contains essential insights regarding what actions one ought to take in the face of adverse circumstances.

Dr. Sidney Kawimbe
Lecturer-Commerce & Business Studies
DMI St Eugene University

CHAPTER ONE

THINK RIGHT

In the Book of Genesis, the Bible documents that man was created by God in His image and likeness. This irrefutable truth should gift you the premise on which to have a positive self-image and a progressive mindset vis-à-vis your life. The fact that you are created in the image of God should suffice in silencing any argument with regard to your identity.

It is gratifying to know that God the creator of all things tangible and intangible knows you by your name. God cares for you and your family and He loves you with an everlasting love. This explains why God wants you to harbor the right thoughts in your mind pertaining to your existence here on earth. Some people erroneously believe that good living is a preserve of the rich and famous. This is a blue lie from the pit of hell. A successful and prosperous life is up for grabs to everyone who wishes to have it. Life in abundance is the will of God for every believer.

The problem with some people today is that they have no motivation to work or do something constructive with their lives. Their minds are set on making 'fast money' disregarding the fact that wealth creation is a process. It is of vital importance to appreciate that there is a process that precedes every good success. That is the reason why I am fervently encouraging you to rise to the occasion and make something out of your life.

I started writing this book when I was still in university. Many people including my fellow students could not believe that I was writing a book and that it was nearly ready for publication. Among my fellow students there was no shortage of cynics and skeptics. Some even questioned my aptitude to write anything worth reading.

One thing I learnt from these naysayers is that some people expect great things to only come from people with high profiles and not from nonentities. With such an attitude, they by the same token debar themselves from success because they presume that they are far from greatness. If you have ambitions to attain greatness, do not discourage and deride other people who equally have similar ambitions. Every person has the potential to achieve great feats in life.

If you think you can succeed in this life, what can stop others from making it too? Do not be self-seeking. Learn to respect and appreciate other people's probabilities in terms of them becoming successful. The race is not for the swift nor the battle for the wise but time and chance happens to them all. The person who you disdain and look down on today maybe you look up to tomorrow.

In life, never underestimate a Christian no matter how dismal their present status might be because God's mighty power is intrinsically at work within them. Therefore, look at every believer using God's perception. God sees potential in every human being not considering of their background and present status.

I must admit that sometimes getting certain things done can prove to be a daunting task. Changing one's mind set is not a walk in the park. A paradigm shift requires a lot of effort and will power but that does not imply that it is an impossible task. Make maximum use of your thought processes to bring about the change that you so desire to see in your life. This is because the mind is a powerful tool that the devil normally uses to bring a spirit of negativity and stagnation in people. The Bibles assertively states that, "as a man thinks in his heart so is he."

The foregoing statement is very factual to all intents and purposes. It defies any logical argument that your success or failure is contingent upon what manner of thoughts you accommodate in your mind. If truth be told, you can never rise above what you think of yourself. You are your own perception index. Your thoughts to a large extent tend to set the parameters for your life.

Some people waste precious time criticizing other people's success because they are given to understand that most affluent people are involved in Satanism. It is true that a lot of successful people are involved in shady deals including involvement in Satanism. But for the sake of our discourse let's draw attention to the fact that our God owns all the silver and gold that is located in every part of the universe. He can bless you with riches beyond your wildest dreams. He can give you above which you can ask, think or imagine according to the power that is at work in you. He is a rich God who reigns from everlasting to everlasting. He created you to carry out the purposes of His Kingdom. He expects you to turn to Him at all times for refuge and comfort.

The late legendary evangelist Billy Graham once said, ***"God loves you so much to leave you the way you are."*** There is a call for you to be what God created you for because He loves you so dearly. We are people of destiny. We find fulfillment in life only when we discover God's plan for our lives and begin to walk in it.

All this may not be making sense to you at the moment but wait a minute. The Bible says to them that believe all things are possible. You are a candidate of God's abundant blessings if you believe you have the mind of God. God is ready and more than willing to lavish you with untold riches. People will be wondering how an ordinary person like you attained such extraordinary prosperity. In case you are not yet born again, accept Jesus as your personal savior then only will this narrative begin to make sense to you.

In view of the foregoing, you can only think right by feeding your mind with the right information. Your mind is a very important part of your being. A properly programmed mind can help you dispel all negative energy around you. You must deliberatively resolve to feed your mind with the word of God. With the word of God entrenched in your psyche, your thoughts will be prone to God. If you continue thinking godly thoughts, you are progressively positioning yourself for greatness. If you consistently believe that you are what the

Bible says you are, you will begin to gravitate towards God ordained prosperity.

Furthermore, your mind can be set on the right-thinking trajectory when you develop a habit of reading Christian motivational books and lending your ears to excellent and inspirational speeches. If you are looking to have a good life, you will have to do yourself a favor by constructing a corresponding mindset. Success often precedes a period of drastic circumstances.

If your mind tells you that something cannot be done, surely nothing will be done. It is as simple as that. Many people are not privy to the fact that it is so easy to get things done. The most important thing to do is to develop a positive intellectual attitude, by disregarding all divergent feeds. What you tell your mind is what your mind will tell you back. Therefore, configure your mind with the word of God and thus apply right-thinking in your activities.

Change the environment

The environment in which you live apparently has a bearing on the way you think. It also plays a critical role in the way you make decisions. By environment I am referring to a matrix of comprising places, people and institutions you are surrounded by and therefore inexorably interact with. It can be argued that there are communities and places where your potential and abilities are never accredited with any importance.

If you find yourself in an antagonistic environment, make every effort to relocate elsewhere in order to avoid aborting your dream. Some places and people are not user friendly to your dream of making it in life. You need to be in an environment that will enhance the prospect of maximizing your potential. As earlier alluded to, the environment you are in somewhat influences your way of thinking and how you interpret the prevailing circumstances.

Some environments may make it practically unattainable for you to make any gainful strides in life. It therefore follows that such environments are contradictions in terms. For example, if you are repeatedly found in the company of individuals whose thinking is not in sync with yours, you must disconnect yourself from such company. Those are signals that you are hanging out with wrong people. Given that pessimism is said to be transmittable, leave such people lest they influence you to start thinking like them. Find an appropriate environment where your mind set and focus will not experience any corruption. Have you ever wondered why you have not pulled off anything of value notwithstanding having great ideas? The answer could be that the environment you are in cannot smooth the progress of your envisioned social and economic uplift. You have all the reasons in this world to run off from such places.

Be careful with some brothers

"Then Joseph had a dream, and when he told it to his brothers, they hated him even more. And he said to them, "please listen to this dream which I have had; for behold, we were binding sheaves in the field, and lo, my sheaf rose up and also stood

erect. Your sheaves gathered around and bowed down to see my sheaf."

(Genesis 37:5-7)

I suppose you have a vision/dream which you are so obsessive about. Let us attempt to define a dream. A dream may simply imply a series of events racing through one's mind while sleep. It may as well connote one's overriding thoughts while either asleep or awake.

Dreams may be ordinary or extraordinary. Ordinary dreams are dreams which may materialize as a consequence of what one experienced during the day. Such dreams may be classified as inconsequential and commonplace. On the contrary, extraordinary dreams are dreams that in all probability are a medium of communication between the dreamer and the Almighty God. They are intended to communicate future events in the life of the dreamer and some specific instructions designed to make the fine points of the dream come to pass.

A case in point is how God communicated with Joseph through dreams. The dreams had filled him with ecstasy. His excitement stemmed from the fact that by implication, Joseph was going to rule over his brothers in future. As a matter of fact, he was going to ascend to a position of greatness, authority and power and was as a consequence going to be served by many.

When Joseph recounted the dream to his brothers, who incidentally already disliked him because of being Jacob's favorite child, the Bible says they even loathed him more. As the saying goes, there was no love lost between Joseph and his envious siblings. It is easy to tell that there was a lot of bad blood between Joseph and his own brothers.

It is astonishing and outrageous how some brothers and sisters from the same family can develop inconceivable sibling rivalry to the point of scheming bloodshed against one another. Jealousy and bitterness form such a strong and lethal permutation that can also pit one family against the other by way of witchcraft. To some this may sound untrue and farfetched. This is Africa; don't forget.

 People will wish you dead and hate you with intensity when you start making it in life. I find it relatively weird that a brother will hate his own brother just because he is on the road to success. Why not just pat him on the back and learn from him how he broke out of the family's generational cycle of poverty. Why entertain thoughts of murder against your very own brother?

There is a lot of irrefutable evidence to the effect that some parents even go to the extent of casting spells on their own children just to prevent them from making it in life. How do you do that to your own genetic offspring? Such practices are satanic and an indignation in God's eyes. Africa must wake up, wise up and thrust aside witchcraft since it is tremendously retrogressive and detrimental. Let the love of God reign in our lives. Love is all we need for each other and not casting spells on your next-door neighbor. Be your brother's keeper for God sake!

Joseph's story points to the fact that God has a way in which He communicates and reveals the plans He has for those that love Him and are called according to His purposes. He communicates so that the dreamer may begin to brace himself for the actualization of the dream. For realization of the dream begins with the dreamer having a strong belief and an appropriate mental attitude.

Everyone has a dream; that one ambition that dominates your mind and your subconscious. A dream is primarily a vision of what you desire to ultimately become in life. It could be a dream of becoming an accountant, a pastor, an entrepreneur or whatever. It is a thought that does not seem to go away, it lingers on in perpetuity!! You may have tried to ignore its promptings but it is engraved in the inner recesses of your heart. The more you try to suppress it, the stronger its pangs become.

Listen! Chances are that it is God who has placed that burning and niggling desire in you. You must be sensitive enough to appreciate that God granted you that particular desire so that you may live a fulfilled and purpose- driven life. Make concerted efforts in avoiding a miscarriage of that dream! God always has destiny helpers lined up along your ordained trajectory of life. Seek guidance from mature Christians. Share your dream with people who will support you; people who will not cast evil incantations upon your dear life or hate you as the case was with Joseph and his begrudging brothers!

Safeguard public properties

One phenomenon that really breaks my heart is the spectacle of young people getting caught up in the motiveless destruction of public property in the name of remonstrating against tangible or superficial government incompetence in handling the affairs of higher institutions of learning and the country at large. It is in the public domain that young people are on a regular basis being used (or abused) by politicians in their expedition to ascend to public office.

It can be assertively stated that in Africa, youths are viewed and employed by powerful politicians as mere instruments of political violence. It is imperative for the youth of any progressive country to have an informed view with regard to the value and significance of public property.

It is within the realm of conjecture that many youths who are hired to fuel public protests, have no inkling how public property is constructed or purchased. They have no idea that public property is funded by taxpayer's money. To home in this point, youths must recognize that public property is made available through taxes paid by their parents, from their hard-earned money. All civilized well-meaning youths must not partake of such retrogressive activities. Use your youthful energy and intellectual property in the furtherance of your country's social and economic development. There are many cultured ways of making your voices of protest heard.

Stop being used as tools for dragging the country backwards by involving yourselves in things which do not even matter. You should bear in mind that it is the community you live in that suffers the consequences of damaged public property. If you are concerned about the development of your country, you should be thinking of ways and means of positively contributing to that cause.

Let me reiterate that you need to be a youth that desires to see development taking place in your country. Seek more and more decent and courteous ways of resolving the many faceted conflicts in the country. In fact, problems and misunderstandings are resolved through dialogue and not by occasioning damage on public property.

You should determine to be a responsible youth and add your voice to the calls for development in your vicinity. You must seriously reflect on issues of prosperity. Think and act in such a manner that the next generation will find a place they will proudly call their country or continent. Future generations deserve to find good infrastructure such as roads, street lights and all those public facilities that give the country a face-lift. Even when you leave this earth, the succeeding generation will hold you in high esteem for having left the country in one piece. Be a youth that thinks about the next generation.

Sometimes it is shocking and disappointing to see high school students participating in the destruction and sabotage of public infrastructure. Instead of vandalizing school properties, find out how the same properties came into existence and how much was spent on them. For goodness sake, be in school for the right reasons and I can assure you that with time, Africa and the world at large will be a better place to live in.

Imagine yourself as a caring father who toils with all your strength to buy household goods for your children's comfort and enjoyment. Alas each time the children have a contentious issue with you they decide to destroy part of that property as a way of registering their grievance against you! What would be your reaction to such a manifestation of ingratitude after spending so much on whatever you bought for them? I am sure you would feel like you have been stabbed in the back. You would feel exceedingly disillusioned to say the least.

The feeling you experience is exactly how the government feels when public property is promiscuously impaired by remonstrating students. I think I have amply belabored the point that violent demonstrations accompanied by vandalism of public property are a counterproductive method of making your position known. There is basically no rationalization for such kind of behavior.

Stay focused

In life it is of the essence for an individual to be diligent, focused and pragmatic as he moves on in his/her life's journey. The above-mentioned aspects are what distinguish achievers from serial failures. Being focused connotes being single-minded, tenacious and steadfast in pursuing one's set goals. A focused person is someone who pays attention to detail and carefully follows the dictates of his envisioned future. His sights are set on the ultimate goal and he does not tolerate disruptions to get his eyes "off the ball". So whatever goals you are pursuing in life, ensure that circumspection is observed.

In life there is no guarantee that things will always be rosy. Life by its very nature comes packaged in varying circumstances. There are highs and lows as well as ups and downs. In view of this, it is very easy for someone's dream to be derailed. The dreamer must hence demonstrate strength of character and presence of mind in order to stay the course.

Ensure that intermittent hostile circumstances do not cause you to lose focus and ultimately fail to attain your goals. Stay away from people who in a subtle manner may be trying to shift your attention from what you are striving to achieve. Be true to yourself and respond to your intrinsic abilities. The Bible says, 'to them that believe, all things are possible.' Commit your plans to God, do the best you can and let God do the rest.

Furthermore, do not be dismayed when you recognize that other people are making it ahead of you. Being persuaded that your time is coming also; celebrate their success and the Lord who knows the motives of every human being will bless you too in due course. Do not be covetous of your friend's success. Relax and continue believing that you are next in line.

The fact that other people are succeeding in their pursuits, is a strong hint that victory is your portion too; provided you remain focused. No matter what comes your way remember to fix your eyes on your objective. Stay resolute and determined. In all these things the bottom line is that in the background, God is stage-managing something for your good. Soon you will reap the rewards of your trust in God if you faint not.

Keep on doing things to the best of your ability. Keep on pushing your agenda until something happens. Do not lose heart when it appears as if your efforts are drawing a blank. Keep expecting. Expectation is the mother of manifestation! Picture yourself as an expectant mother who is determined to give birth in the face of imminent labor pains.

She is ready to endure birth pangs because of her love for the unborn child. Her love for the forthcoming child by far outstrips the pain contained in the process she will unavoidably experience. She gives birth because her joy lies in seeing her child being born. She eventually births the child because it is every woman's desire to be a mother.

That is why you should not just watch the clock; do what it does. Its hands are ever on the move! Do what you have to do in order to have what you want to have. Do not be quick to throw in the towel yet. It is not over until God says it is over! Narrow your focus on your desired expectation.

Be willing and strong enough to confront whatever life throws at you. Never give up and never give in. Look forward to the future with bated breath. Your current socio-economic status does not determine your ultimate quality of life. Keep your vision alive in spite of intermediate bottlenecks. Endure every adversity that you meet along the road to success. It is never an easy road.

You have what it takes

But David said to Saul, "your servant has been keeping his father's sheep. When a lion or bear came and carried off a sheep from the flock, I went after it, struck it and rescued the sheep from its mouth. When it turned on me, I seized it by its hair, struck it and killed it. Your servant has killed both the lion and the bear; this uncircumcised philistine will be one of them, because he has defied the armies of the living God. The Lord who delivered me from the paw of the lion and the paw of the bear will deliver me from the hands of this philistine."

(1 Samuel 17:34-37)

The story of David makes very interesting reading. It is an extremely inspiring and heartening narrative. In the eyes of people, David came across as an ordinary boy like any other. As such, people in his neighborhood treated him like everyone else. His father knew him as a good shepherd boy looking after family sheep. In other words, David was given common treatment because no one apart from God was cognizant of his imminent position.

No one has the faintest idea of the intrinsic abilities of this little shepherd boy. No one could discern that each time they looked at him they were effectively looking at the future king of Israel. Going by his appearance, he was regarded as just an inconsequential rural community guy.

It is wrong to judge a book by its cover. People may ascribe an erroneous profile to you because they are not privy to what God has configured in your inner life. In such cases, it is important to recognize your intrinsic abilities and patiently wait for an opportune moment to showcase to the whole world what you are really made of. There will come a time when you will be celebrated for your exploits. The people who now say "who are you" will that time say "how are you sir."

The story of David and Goliath also teaches us great lessons with reference to our veiled competences. There was a time when the entire army of Israel was afraid of a man named Goliath. He was a giant of a man who defied the entire battalion of the army of Israel. It is recorded that Goliath insulted and challenged King Saul and his army to fight him. Unfortunately, no one from the camp of Israel had the valor and audacity to take up the challenge.

Clearly this was a desperate situation for King Saul and his army. However, in *1 Samuel 17:34-37* we read how David rose to the occasion and against all odds confronted the situation with boldness, courage and faith. When David got wind of the intimidations and insults hurled at the Israeli army by Goliath, he knew he could put an end to the giant's hecklings.

He was persuaded in his spirit that he could make a difference based on his past experiences with God in the bush, as he went about tending sheep. So, David told Saul of what the Lord had done through him. He explained how he slew a lion and the bear to protect the sheep. Obviously, his triumph over these two lethal wild animals had emboldened him a great deal!

To cut a long story short, David, to the annoyance of all and sundry offered to not only to antagonize Goliath the titanic Philistine, but to exterminate him by cutting off his head; like he did to the lion and the bear. David knew what he was talking about and he exhibited totally no fright of the towering the Philistine.

 David knew deep down his heart he was spiritual giant in the Lord. He had faith that the Lord who previously delivered him from the paw of the lion and the bear would surely deliver Goliath into his hands. **You have what it take**s in this life to confront challenges and win for that is your faith and confidence in God and His word. You need challenges in life and when they come, you face them with an upbeat mindset. It does not matter how big the challenges are but what you can do. Respond to them with faith and an attitude of triumph

CHAPTER TWO
HAVE FAITH AND HOPE

"And now abides faith, hope and love, these three but the greatest of these is love."

(Corinthians 13:13)

From the scripture above, we understand that faith, hope and love are eternal, and they abide forever. This means everything a man does in faith, hope and love has eternal value. Anything that is done in these three virtues is recognized in heaven before God. But He said that love is the greatest of the three. This is because love encompasses both faith and hope **(Galatians 5:6).** The Bible says that faith works by love. For faith to work effectively you must walk in love. The Bible says that hope does not disappoint because of love **(Romans 5:5).**

"Hope does not disappoint us, because God has poured out His love into our hearts by the Holy Spirit whom He has given us."

(Romans 5:5)

Hope is for tomorrow. Hope has the image of the future; it always sees the future. Hope is very important in life; without it you can't really fight for anything or pursue anything in life. This is because without hope there is no future. Without hope there is no vision and where there is no vision people perish. Hope gives ability to see the future and the strength and tenacity to pursue the future seen in hope. Hope gives endurance and patience. Armed with hope, you can endure any adversity or pessimistic circumstances until you see the vision come to pass. Men of hope never give up or give in, they stand their ground.

It is advisable on no account to drop optimism in life. If for any reason you are losing grip of your hope in life, just fall back on the word of God. The word is a fountain of hope in any event. Remember to pray; especially by using the word of God as the basis for your prayers. Hold on to that hope even if it is by the skin of your teeth. Let me say it again, never give up.

Hope comes through the gospel of Christ. When a person hears the gospel of Christ, hope and faith begins to take form in his heart.

"Now faith is the substance of things hope for the evidence of things not seen."

(Hebrews 11:1)

Faith is the substance of things hoped for. This is a powerful statement indeed! Faith shrouds your hope with substance. This implies that faith brings the future into the present setting. Faith is a 'now' attribute, while hope is for all intents and purposes futuristic.

On the other hand, faith introduces the things you hope to see in the future today. Hope says you will have it, whereas faith says you have it now though you can't see or feel it. Faith is the assurance (the confirmation, the title deed) of things hope for. Faith is the guarantee, the title deed to indicate that you now have the things you hope for.

The latter part of the scripture above says "faith is the evidence of the things not seen". From a legal perspective, the term "evidence" is one and the same with proof. Faith is the proof of the things not seen. By extension, this means faith does not strive to get something; faith by and in itself is the proof that whatsoever things you hope for are yours now.

Just like love and hope, figuratively speaking, faith has sight. Love sees the best in everybody because the Bible says it covers a multitude of sins and does not keep a record of wrongs. Love sees the prospective integrity in someone.

Hope also sees. Like love, the eyes of hope are in the heart of man. Hope sees the desired future. It has the propensity to visualize how things will pan out in the future. Faith too has sight and sees from the heart. Faith perceives realities which cannot be perceived by human faculties. A case in point is when you get born again, the Holy Spirit abides in and with you; and yet you cannot see Him with your naked eyes. However, you can see Him through the eyes of faith as He is epitomized in the word of God.

Love is everlasting, hope is futuristic and faith is in the present tense. These three principles are of the essence constituting the foundations upon which you must secure your life.

"Remembering without ceasing your work of faith, and labor of love, and patience of hope in our Lord Jesus Christ in the sight of God and our Father."

(1 Thessalonians 1:3)

The Bible does allude to the labor of love, a theme which borders on the work of faith and the endurance or patience of hope. This encompasses everything you do out of love, every labor of love and the work of your faith. The work of your faith refers to your deeds and the words you speak in line with the word of God. The list may include the endurance and patience you exhibit in your heart due to the hope you derive from the word of God. These are the works which are accepted before God.

If you have a dream in life, season it with hope, faith and love. Allow the word of God to feed into and inform your life. Have hope for tomorrow and have faith for victorious life now. Ensure that everything you do it in love and as unto the Lord. The Bible says in no uncertain terms that love is the most excellent way of doing things.

This is the surest way of achieving lasting and inclusive success in life. You and I are aware that there is success with men and success with God. The God kind of success is eternal considering that its impact is felt in this age and in the age to come.

Do not worm your way to the top in a fraudulent manner. Do not use egotism as your motivation and inducement for wanting to succeed in life. Desist from taking corruption as you spur to riches. Remember there is a way that seems right to every man and the end result is death. Everything that is not done in faith is not of God. Without God as our sure foundation, we are building on sinking sand. The building will utterly fall and its fall will predictably be great.

Success does not consist in the abundance of the material belongings we may own. Good and true success consists in fulfilling God's purposes for your life and establishing the trajectory to your destiny. Success requires you to be located at the right place and at the right time for your life to resonate with God's purposes. Legitimate success is in rooted in the word of God.

Let Love, hope and faith conduct you all the way to your position of divine appointment. By so doing, God will be with you in all you do every step of the way. While you are at it, remember that with faith even as little as mustard seed, all things are possible. All things are possible to them that believe. This means when you persuasively believe something, you have brought that belief into the realm of possibility. It becomes achievable, attainable and feasible. The beauty of being a child of God is that you always move under an open window of opportunities and potential. We believe the word of God because it is quick, alive and sharper than a two-edged sword.

This should give you the valor and audacity to do what may seem impracticable. This issue should embolden you to confront intractable and depressing circumstances that often attempt to put a wedge between us and our preferred expectations. In this life, never give up on your dreams and never write off anybody even if they appear to be headed nowhere! People are the most precious creatures on earth. Do not ever be under the misguided notion that materials have more value than your fellow human being.

CHAPTER THREE
VALUE PEOPLE

We are all part of each other's existence, at least in the philosophical sense. Every person you come across is a product of God's love. You exist because of God's love and that also can be said about other people. We are all equal in the sight of God. God attaches equal magnitude to every human being.

Though the Bible implies that money answers all things, we should not commit the appalling error of rating money above people. The essence of our being blessed is that we should be a blessing to others. Furthermore, having appropriated salvation, we should neither judge nor condemn those who have not yet responded to God's love. God is love and we are all obligated to love and esteem others.

If we are going to be fittingly associated with name of Jesus, we should value one another, knowing that we are all part of God's big plan for mankind. Every person you interact with is equally part of God's scheme of things.

We meet different kinds of people on a daily basis. Each person we meet has a face which tells a story. Our contacts interface with us to be helped or to help us. Others are placed into our lives for the purpose of a common cause such as business partnerships. Others are strategically positioned at various intersections our lives to teach us how to succeed.

David lived in the palace in order to learn the conventions and protocols of the palace. He also developed a bond with the king's son which later helped him greatly when the king was after his life. The son of the king facilitated David's deliverance.

The People in our lives are very important factors. People are God's channel for bringing dreams to reality. God does not have physical hands and legs. God will render His help through the people He has positioned in your life. When we talk about open doors we are actually making direct reference to people.

In life take friendships and acquaintances seriously. The person you despise the most could be a boon to steer you to success that is beyond your wildest dream. The worst thing you could ever do is to look down on others. Your circle of friends has more consequence than you give it credit for.

Going back to my high school days, I wonder where my classmates from rich families are at. Where are those who labeled you a dunderhead for obtaining disgraceful grades? Where are those big brains to which Mathematics, Chemistry and Physics were a walk over?

You probably are living a better life than them. Life has a way of leveling the social topography. If you look gaze in the rear-view mirror of your life, you will surely be grateful to God for the progress you have registered. If you were to ask me, all I can say is that God is great and merciful.

When it seemed, there was no glimmer of optimism, He came through for me. When some naysayers thought I was a spent force, God renewed my strength and set me on a solid rock. He has blessed me with good health and true happiness. Today I can eat whatever I want. I therefore challenge you to never to have a pitiable self-esteem. You are unique and valued by God; who made you in His own image and likeness.

A human being is by default the temple of God. It is therefore an affront to God's intelligence when we despise and underrate any human being. The person you call a riff raff today will be a president tomorrow. The very neighbor who infuriatingly keeps asking for salt and mealie meal could be your knight in shining armor tomorrow. That's the way it is!

Only God knows the destiny of each one of us. Be careful with the way you profile people; their tomorrow may leave you speechless! The people who are struggling to make ends meet today could be the next employers of your children and your grandchildren. Life is full of surprises.

What God has done for others He can do for you too. The crux of the matter is that everyone has the potential to make it in life. It is a grave mistake to classify, define and judge people by their present particulars. When their time and opportunity present itself, they shall prosper and their shame will take a bow. Every believer in God is a millionaire in waiting.

As long as the power of God lives inside them, anything is possible. That's why it's very important to give respect even to your own workers. You don't know what they will become tomorrow.

Dear employer,

Human resource is a vital constituent to an organization that needs to be respected. An organization or business runs smoothly because of its employees. The success of every business is dependent on the morale and motivation of its members of staff. Employees must be treated with dignity and respected in order for their productivity and efficiency to increase. Mutual respect between employers and employees is huge necessity.

Motivation can be through verbal appreciation, monetary form and good working conditions. Motivation means different things to different people. Some employees feel valued when their employers find time to talk to them one on one. Before you start calling an employee all sorts of names regarding their performance, try to talk to them as a human resource manager. You may find out exactly what makes them inefficient at work. Remember you cannot be a supervisor without employees.

One of the best ways to grow your business is to invest in your employees. Employees are your eyes and ears. They see and hear what you are not privy to. As employees they are your representatives hence the need for opportune empowerment by you. If your employees are not fully equipped with up to date intellectual capital, your business may decline or eventually collapse.

Many businesses collapse upon the death of the founder. This is so because many business owners don't invest in their employees. Management scholars have proved that intangible assets such as human capital are a great necessity for a corporate entity to survive in the ever-changing business environment.

CHAPTER FOUR
STEP UP YOUR GAME

Each year thousands of students are graduating with undergraduate and post graduate educational qualifications. Times have changed compared to 50 years ago when we had only a few graduates particularly in Zambia. In Zambia there is at least one university in each province.

Years back, only the rich could afford a cell phone. But today, even a 12 years old child owns a smart phone. Times have really changed and knowledge has significantly increased. Technology on the other hand is moving at a faster rate than before. The World has developed into a global village largely due to advancements in travel, communication and information technology. We no longer live the way we used to leave 20 years ago. The quality of life has improved as well life expectancy.

There have been many talking points vis-à-vis communication technology, particularly social media. Both parents and different governments across the globe have raised concerns about the way young people are abusing social media. The social media technology has been received with mixed feelings.

The truth is; we haven't seen anything yet! There is more sophisticated technology being constructed as we speak. These days of increase in knowledge are foretold in the Bible.

The technology has its pros and cons. As believers, let us use it in the dissemination of the gospel of Jesus Christ.

Notwithstanding the public discourse about social media, technology has come to ease our way of doing things. Instead of the conventional post office mail system, we now send mail electronically. One can now access information in the twinkling of an eye by using Google search engine for example. Instead of a telegram we can now chart on WhatsApp, Messenger, SMs, Face book and through many more technological innovations.

It is true that some people are using this technology for the wrong reasons. But to others, it is a platform for doing business. I know some prominent business experts who are using social media to teach young people principles of investment and other entrepreneurial skills. While abuse is going on, others have exploited social media to great positive effect. Social media is bad or good depending on which spectacles you are viewing it with.

Abandon mediocrity

The fact that life offers each one of us an opportunity or opportunities defies any logical argument. With the increase of knowledge and technology, it is incumbent upon an individual to choose what to do with it. We are all at liberty to choose whatever we feel is best for our lives. Many things are at our disposal but we have to exercise discretion and discernment.

I would be interested to know what young people are using the internet for. Of course, many are using it to watch pornographic videos and watching online sex.

If you are a youth and you happen to using social media for worthless pursuits, I would urge to stop being mediocre and wise up. The people you are busy slighting on social media are probably living a high standard of life while you are busy wasting your data bundles on vanity.

There is so a lot you can achieve with the gift of communication you are using to slur people. Needless to mention, the insults you keep on posting will not take you anywhere. Some of the people you insult are old enough to be your fathers and grandfathers. Be respectful. Additionally, you must come to your senses and realize that you need to use the internet for constructive purposes. Ensure your name is not on the catalog of abusers of social media.

Students are graduating from a variety of institution of higher education in massive numbers every year. The rate at which people are acquiring advanced educational qualifications is heartwarming. However, the failure by many of these graduates to deliver according to their qualifications is a source of concern. Having a degree is a good thing but competence in applying that intellectual capital is of the essence.

The substantiation and efficacy of your being educated is epitomized by the way you apply the knowledge you acquired from school. You cannot claim to have a Degree in Marketing but fall short of conceptualizing a simple advertisement. It is within the realm of conjecture that you possibly obtained your degree suspiciously. If you cannot be influenced to think in line with what you have been taught in school, then learning has not taken place. It's as simple as that. You cannot claim to be a Mathematician when you cannot tabulate simple arithmetic.

You must always disassociate yourself from mediocrity. Make concerted efforts to ensure that you are not living below your God given potential. There is a lot you can do with your computer or your writing skills. Living below par when you can do wonders with your abilities is an affront to God who gifted you the abilities.

Everything good you do even at your place of work is accompanied by a delight effect. Excellence will always earn you a good appraisal by your boss. One important thing worth repeating is that things have changed over the time. The way organizations used to keep records has changed radically. People and companies are now going green. Organizations and individuals have to keep abreast with new technology and to embrace it. Ensure that you keep tabs on what is constantly evolving in the sphere of technology. Be media savvy for the sake of the kingdom. We are not going backwards but moving forward. Change with the time albeit without compromising your Christianity.

CHAPTER FIVE
WHO IS YOUR BUYER?

People tend to put the blame on the people they interact with for why things occur in a certain way. The people we meet and surround ourselves with are a reflection of what we are. Our acquaintances are what defines us and points to where we are headed in life. The people we hang out with are who we are! That is why we must choose our inner circle of friends carefully fully aware that bad company spoils good morals. Ask yourself if the friends you have are good material for enhancing your personal social and economic development.

To my sisters

Allow me to appreciate God for your beauty which is by all accounts indisputable. Your splendor is in fact a manifestation of God's ingenuity and artistic ability. Your loveliness was borne out by God causing Adam to sleep in the Garden of Eden in order to engineer such a masterpiece called a woman. Today men still glance at you and are mesmerized by God's inventiveness. To God be the Glory for your exquisiteness.

All things considered, a woman occupies a special place in society. She is held in high esteem in many respects. In view of this, a woman is expected to carry herself with clearly identifiable dignity in the public eye. Her conduct must be commensurate with respect and aura attached to womanhood. Putting all this in perspective, society's expectations of a woman are extremely high. The bar set for her conduct is extraordinarily lofty. The ideal dynamics of a woman are certainly out of this world.

The conduct and wardrobe of a woman are always under public scrutiny. The value attached to a woman is what demands her to be respected. Above and beyond every other consideration, a woman is a life giver. We are all born of a woman and that's an area of expertise exclusively ascribed to womenfolk.

However, the high expectations placed on a woman are in many cases not fulfilled. Some women (mainly girls) have chosen to take a different path altogether, contradicting the criteria set for a decent woman. This has led to loss of respect for the woman. Women who are supposed to be the conscience of society have desecrated their high standing. Suddenly we are left to ask these questions: what has happened to the self-respect of women? Why have they left their area of strength? What happened to the dignity they are known for?

The real beauty of a woman lies in her virtuousness. Real beauty is in intangible form. Being attractive doesn't mean walking in the streets half naked as is the case of many girls today. A few equally depraved men may fall for such morally degenerate women. It is no longer a big deal nowadays to see girls with exposed breasts, thighs and clad in body-hugging see-through attire. No man in his right frame of mind can seriously contemplate marrying a woman who is not ashamed of indecent exposure. Please ladies dress up modestly and maintain the conventional values of a woman!

You will identify a certain product either by a logo on it or a trade mark. A product is distinguished from other products by its branding. Branding simply means to make your product look different from other products already on the market. It requires strategic planning to ensure that a product is perfectly advertised to its end users. The manufacturer has the reaction of a potential customer in mind when conceptualizing the branding. Branding is a very important part of marketing because it ensures that a product is abundantly distinguishable from other products. The product must not be mistaken for another product already on the market.

Anything can sell depending on the place, the price and the person buying. In fact, every product manufactured is designed to meet a need. The lady's wings and creams for bleaching the skin are a result of someone's thinking. Those who bleach their skin, someone sat down and came up with the formula in order to meet their perspective (brand) about life. The people behind the product had already their potential buyers and consumers in the picture. You are a brand that attracts the intended consumer. As a lady what kind of a man are you attracting?

As a lady, the way you carry yourself speaks louder than you think. Do not become a subject of public discourse in a negative way, of course. Do not give people a reason to call you a woman of ill-repute. Avoid taking beauty to a level that is disagreeable and contemptible. You have the right to look your very best but not at the expense of your dignity and natural respect. Look good and smell good, but remain a respectable and acceptable brand. Above and beyond, embrace the values and the respect that is credited to a woman. Society's expectations of an ideal woman are very high. Ensure you do not lower that bar. You are the mother of your neighborhood and that includes men. Don't play the villain or harlot.

In spite of everything you are still special

There is no carbon copy of you here on the earth. There will never be another you ever. No wonder everyone's DNA is different. That makes you very special and unique in the sight of God.

Perhaps you have been involved in despicable immoral activities and feel you are beyond redemption. You can rest assured that you cannot go too far in sin for the grace of God to fail to catch up with you. You are not too lost to be found. God loves you more than you will ever know. There is absolutely no sin too big to be forgiven and forgotten. That is the language of the devil! Allow God to rebrand you with a brand-new name and a new standard of living. The ball is in your court! God is ready when you are!

Don't commit suicide

Being alive on this planet is an exciting time. As long as we are alive opportunities to make amends and serve God are accessible. Though you may be weighed down by the intolerable pressures of this life, there is always hope beyond the horizon.

If you are contemplating committing suicide, think of people you know who had similar problems but managed to weather the storm and are enjoying life again. Your problem is not special. Everyone has a fair share of challenges and nothing should make you think you have a lion's share.

Suicide is a selfish act. It is a function of self-centeredness. Imagine of the people who may get hurt and get unendingly traumatized as a result of taking your own life. There are many examples of people who suffered big losses in their lives but endured the pain and shame. Today they are back on their feet again.

One of the worst things you could ever do as an individual is to give up as a result of the innumerable failures. Jesus never came for the perfect. He came for the sick, the downcast, the poor and all those who are consigned to the outer reaches of society.

If there is anybody who feels your pain, rejection, self-pity and distress it can only be Jesus. Jesus took your trouble on the cross thus you should not continue perishing. Don't needlessly cut your life short because God can use your circumstances as stepping stone for success. Your mess can become a message of hope for many other lives.

To the society/the church

Christians are meant to live for each other. The way we treat others reflects the level of relationship we have with God. We can only love certain people with the love of God, agape or unconditional love.

As a consequence, you cannot proclaim that you love God whom you do not see and dislike intensely the person you see. You and I probably have had occasion to delete certain people from our circle of friends. Others have been rejected by their family members for different reasons. But who is without sin? We all have sinned and fallen short of the glory of God.

The church on the other hand is called to be a dispensary of God's love. The true love of God is measured by how we treat those who have messed up their lives. The church should ensure that those who feel rejected by society come to realization that there is a God who cares about them and does not condemn them.

It is a pity that today there are church people who are in the forefront in criticizing and condemning those who have fallen. The church is not there to rub it in but to provide solace and counseling, in the hope of spiritually rehabilitating such people.

If we are to grow as a church, we need to truly allow the love of God to reign in our lives. Let people know that God lives in us by the way we treat them in spite of their sin blemished life. The role of the church is to spread the good news of the gospel, in so doing providing hope for the hopeless. Now, if the church is perceived to be rejecting people based on their past mistakes, who then will accept them in keeping with the love of God?

Some people avoid going to church because they feel condemned by the church; which should be not the case. The church must serve as a spiritual hospital, admitting people with diverse spiritual maladies.

To parents

Every child has got the potential to make it in life through determined parental guidance. Children need to be taught the word of God at their formative stage of life. Nothing can replace the role of the word in grooming and shaping a child for ultimate greatness.

The child that you believe will amount to nothing could be the one to deliver you from the many challenges you are facing as a parent. Be careful the way you treat your children including other dependents. In the fullness of time, every child can be successful provided they are given good care and direction by their parents and custodians.

Parents are called to raise their children in the fear of the Lord God Almighty. You can discipline your children without any need for name calling. If in anger you give your child a bad name, you are in essence pronouncing a self-fulfilling prediction.

Some children become so aberrant and irredeemable because their parents use very draconian disciplinary methods. Speak the truth to your child in love and not with a belligerent approach. The best way to win back your child is to ensure that you don't sound judgmental and reproachful. Ensure that the problem is handled in a mature way and with sobriety.

Raise a boy child with respect

Who is training and raising a boy child? Who is ensuring that a boy child is taught to respect a woman? Gender based violence against women could be a tale-tell sign that the boy child is not being taught that a woman should be respected and unconditionally loved by her husband. The responsibility that comes with manhood is usually never inculcated or imparted in the mind of a boy child. This could probably be the clarification for the prevalence of domestic sadism predominantly wife battering in homes.

If issues pertaining to gender-based violence are to be addressed and dealt with certainty, parents and other concerned parties, must ensure that a boy child is accorded appropriate points of reference regarding how to take care of a woman. It can be argued that boys are seldom mentored to grow into conscientious men. It is safe to say men learn things by themselves and this trend leaves much to be desired.

The negligence of not preparing a boy child for the demands of manhood can be quantified in the disquieting rate of recurrence of domestic gender-based violence against women. There are many non-governmental organizations which have come on board as advocates and activists for the rights of the girl child. There have been some educational reforms tailored solely for the girl child. A case in point is the re-entry policy for school girls who become pregnant.

But it is quite concerning that the counseling of a boy child is palpably overlooked. How about a boy child who impregnates a girl child? A boy child is always involved unless otherwise. There is a need to educate a boy child on issues regarding early pregnancies. This is food for thought.

Some of the vices some non-government organizations are trying to stop are as a consequence of a boy child not having the requisite awareness. There is so much activism in ensuring the wellbeing of a girl child. All eyes and ears have been predominantly on the girl child. But we should bear in mind that as long as a boy child is subtracted from this social equation, problem will remain a mere talking point, without finding a credible and lasting solution.

CHAPTER SIX
THE NEED FOR JESUS

Jesus Christ paid the ultimate price by dying on the cross to purchase your liberty from the power of sin. He who knew no sin became sin so that we may become the righteousness of God. Furthermore, Jesus became poor so we could become rich. He willingly endured pain and shame on the cross just to guarantee your inheritance in the Kingdom of God. As a matter of fact, He no longer calls you a servant, but friend. He is a friend who sticks closer that a brother!

His love for you is so profound to the extent that He has made boundless provisions for you to enjoy abundant life here on earth. Jesus Christ sacrificed the trappings of heaven to come and die a cruel and humiliating death on the cross just for you. Through His death you and I have been redeemed and delivered from all manner of oppression, including sin. This information should make you forever grateful and highly beholden to Him.

What is it that is depriving you of peace of mind and always making your life a living hell? I have good news for you. I can boldly declare that Jesus is the panacea for all your emotional, spiritual and material needs and wants. In all probability, you will never know what you are missing in life if you do not take serious steps to come to the saving knowledge of Jesus Christ.

Our featured scripture in this chapter is so clear and to the point concerning the promises and intentions of God for your life. It does not matter what your particular circumstances may be in your life. God can change your story in an instant.

You must be tired of feeding on the devil's falsehood. Let me underscore the fact that the devil has a whole range of evil intent against your life. He has misled a lot of people because he comes camouflaged as an angel of light. That is the meaning of the name 'Lucifer'. Without Jesus in your life, you will always remain a sitting target for the devil's malevolent schemes.

 The fact that the devil is a malefactor cannot be overemphasized! With the view of counteracting God's good plans for your life, the devil continues to devise wicked plans over your life. You have the opportunity of your life to access the perfect and good will of God by surrendering your life to Jesus.

There is only one way to spiritual freedom, it is Jesus. He is the way, the truth and the light. He is the only highway to freedom! Jesus came that we might have life and life in abundance. Stop dithering and vacillating between two opinions. Come to Jesus and you will experience the jubilation of a transformed life.

"As he approached the town gate, a dead person was being carried out-the only son of his mother, and she was a widow. And a large crowd from the town was with her. When the Lord saw her, his heart went out to her and he said, "don't cry." then he went up and touched the bier they were carrying him on, and the bearers stood still. He said, "Young man, I say to you, get

up!" the dead man sat up and began to talk, and Jesus gave him back to his mother."

(Luke 7:12-14)

I am trying so hard to make you realize the need to accept Jesus as your personal Savior. Do the right thing by saying yes to Jesus. Let me reiterate the fact that there is totally nothing impossible with Christ Jesus. The gist of **Luke 7:12-14** is that Jesus has the power and authority over anything, which includes death.

The underlying principle is that anything that has a name bows to the name that is above all names; the name of Jesus. Associating yourself with Him will bring a revolutionary change in your life as He resurrects all dead situations in your life. It is imperative for you to see the need for Jesus to intervene in your life.

He is not constrained by the intensity of your challenges. He is the master of all situations and nothing is complicated with Him. I am cheerfully beseeching you to join the growing ranks of born again, Spirit filled believers. Don't be an outsider; become a role player in the Kingdom of God.

"This is what the LORD says- you're Redeemer, the Holy One of Israel: I am the LORD your God, who teaches you what is best for you, who directs you in the way you should go."

(Isaiah 48:17)

Are you at the crossroads of life with no clue regarding which route to take? Do not despair. There is a redeemer who knows what is in your best interest. He chose you before the foundations of the earth and predestined you to accomplish a specific purpose.

Call upon Him and He will instantly answer you and meet you at your point of need. Make Him the center of your life and He will direct your paths. His word shall be a light unto you path and a lamp unto your feet. This will enable you to see where you are going and where you are stepping. He will lead you to your destiny without fail!

Once you let Jesus come into your life, you will fail to comprehend the victories that shall follow. You will not see the exigency of coming to Jesus if in the first instance you do not perceive the necessity to do so. Satan has blinded a lot of people so that they fail to see the need to renounce their sins and come to Jesus. To see the need for Jesus Christ in your life is crucial in the salvation design of God.

As you push forward in this life, fix your eyes on Jesus and your mind on the cross. Then God will see you through all the changeable circumstances of life. You will always take courage knowing that Jehovah is in control.

CHAPTER SEVEN
<u>MAINTAIN YOUR STANCE</u>

"Problems are not stop signs, they are guidelines."

-Robert H. Schuller

In the course of our lives here on earth, tough times have come and gone. Harsh and difficult moments have often proved to be the line of distinction between those who make it in life and those who give up even before the final whistle is blown. In the grand scheme of things, adverse times will always be part of the matrix of life. But the good news is that we have a helper in Jesus.

Remember that quitters do not win and winners do not quit. Before you consider quitting, consider how far you have come. Oh yes! Think of how much energy and resources you have put in your pursuits to give up now. Every difficulty has an expiry date. Quitting is a word that should not exist in your terminology.

Endurance is often the difference between success and failure. Some people lack the vital tenacity to fight to the end and the capacity to wait patiently. It is rightly said that good things come to those who wait. Do not allow prevailing hostile conditions to readjust your focus. Maintain your stance and self-confidence. In the pursuance of your dream you will be bombarded by inauspicious happenings but keep pressing on until you accomplish your mission. Do not be moved or detracted by detrimental circumstances. Be strong and courageous. Keep on pushing and pushing until heaven answers you.

Let us be metaphorical by taking parallels from the game of football. Players only leave the pitch when the referee blows the final whistle. Before that, it is game on! As long as the final whistle has not been sounded, the team that is trailing continues playing to the whistle. They keep on making attempts at the opponent's goal; a sign of keeping their hopes alive.

We have witnessed a team that was seemingly headed for defeat come from behind and win the game in very spectacular if not fascinating circumstances. As long as you are in the will of God, you can rest assured that your story will have a happy ending. When a challenge comes your way, just remember that as a child of God endowed with His power, you shall be equal to the task. The Lord is a mighty and strong tower, the righteous run into it and they are safe.

Life is not for wimps or crybabies. Life is for men and women of courage and strong will. It calls for men and women who stand their ground and refuse to surrender their values and convictions even in the face of adversity. Good and abundant living is available to the sons and daughters of the living God; who know for sure that God is their provider and sustainer. The Bible says those that know their God shall be strong and do great exploits.

It is common knowledge that while here on earth, Jesus passed through a lot of turmoil and adversities of all kinds. He was reviled and rejected by the very people he had come to save. But still, He did not abandon the assignment the Father in heaven had given Him to do. Jesus had a revelation of what was to emerge at the culmination of His task. He endured the ridicule and heightened name calling. He held on to His dream; a dream to save the world through His vicarious death on the cross!

God has remarkable plans and thoughts about His children and that includes you. They are not plans to harm you but to prosper you and to give you a future; and an expected end. To recap what the Bible says, the path of the just is like a shining light that shines brighter and brighter unto that perfect day. So, do not give up. Hold on to your dream because the sun will shine again in your life. Weeping may endure for a night, but joy comes in the morning.

Stagger not at the promises of God over your life. Maintaining a standpoint for what you believe in is a necessary virtue. Standing firm regarding your convictions is the mark of a man of boldness and integrity. Due to lack of spiritual sensitivity and lack of persistence, many people have abandoned their dreams without sensing that their miracle was just around the corner. The desires you have in your heart were given to you by God and the self-same God will make them come to pass.

In the time of hopelessness

Life is a package of varying circumstances; it is decidedly unpredictable. It is an array of times and seasons. Some people easily get discouraged in their season of adversity. It is of vital importance to view challenges from a spiritual perspective.

Adversity is your university. Learn what God is saying in those moments of hopelessness. Storms do not last forever and as a matter of fact there is a blessing in the storm. I once heard that there are no hopeless situations but hopeless people. In times of hopelessness trust in the Lord with everything in you! Jesus is our blessed hope.

"Call to me and I will answer you and tell you great and unsearchable things you do not know."

(Jeremiah 33:3)

Many people make impulsive and ridiculous choices during desperate situations. It is prudent to remain composed even when things are in disarray. Many people have lived to rue the flawed decisions they made out of rage and anxiety. The choices you make today will have a bearing on your tomorrow. Learn how to handle pressure so that you don't lose it! Never allow dire situations and circumstances to override your better judgment.

Some Christians have ended up consulting witch doctors and spirit mediums in their time of desperation. This is a travesty of Christianity. Others have ended up divorcing their spouses because of failing to process and make sense of their seasons of adversity.

*Jeremiah 33:3*clearly indicates that God is so mindful about His creation here on earth. He has made an open invitation to whosoever will; to call on Him at any time. He is ready to answer and reveal great and unsearchable things. Commit your plans to Him and He will surely establish them. God loves you more than you will ever know. He wants you to be in His presence regularly so that communication is constant and stable. In everything you do consult your maker. In fact, He is the best consultant you can ever deal with.

What is blocking you from crossing over?

I wish to draw you back to the story of the children of Israel regarding how they crossed the Red Sea. The story depicts the amazing and wondrous deeds of God. After Pharaoh succumbed to God's pressure to let the Israelites go, he later regretted having made that decision. So, the Egyptian army was sent to go and recapture the Israelites. As the army was pursuing them, the children of Israel needed to cross the Red Sea with urgency. The Egyptian army was fast advancing, hot on their heels. This was on all accounts a desperate moment for them. But the beauty of this story is that God made a way for them where there seemed to be no way. God phenomenally parted the Red Sea and the Israelites crossed as if on dry ground.

"And God Said, "let the water under the sky be gathered to one place, and let dry ground appear." And it was so."

(Genesis 1:6)

In the verse captioned above, God who made the dry ground appear after gathering the waters to one place. Now there came a time to demonstrate that anything created by Him obeys His voice. To cut the story short, the children of Israel walked on dry ground, a sign that nothing is impossible with God.

Impossibility only exists in the mind of man and not God. There is no place of impracticality in God. He makes things which are not as if they were. He is an omniscient God and in consequence He is not subject to any limitations. That is why He has the divine audacity to dare you to ask for anything with the promise that it will be granted. In the final analysis, be unruffled in times of impossibility and let **Jeremiah 33:3**become rhema in your situation.

CHAPTER EIGHT
<u>WORRY AND ANXIETY</u>

"This is why I tell you not to be worried about the food and drink you need in order to stay alive, or about cloths for your body. After all, isn't life worth more than food? And isn't the body worth more than cloths? Look at the birds; they do not sow seeds, gather a harvest and put it in barns; yet your father in heaven takes care of them! Aren't you worth much more than birds? Can any of you live a bit longer by worrying about it?"

(Mathew 6:25-27)

Worry is a very interesting phenomenon. It simply means to be concerned or troubled about something that has happened or is yet to unfold. Naturally we tend to worry about what tomorrow will bring. Every day we are confronted by exigent situations that are a source of worry.

To put it explicitly, there is no shortage of worrisome situations in this world. There are so many dynamics that conspire in making us worry day in and day out. We are all victims of social and economic problems. Even strong Christians are not spared the impact of the harsh economy accompanied by austerity measures.

The word of God implores us not to worry or fret about all these events. What is important is put all these things into perspective by reiterating what the word of God says with regard to worry and anxiety.

59

Our takeaway or conjecture from **Mathew 6:25-27** is that God is responsible for ensuring that anything we desire is provided. He is known as Jehovah Jireh our provider. God will not allow you to live in lack.

Worrying about what to eat, drink and wear is indicative of your lack of trust in God. Worrying is the converse of having faith in God. In fact, it is in difficult moments when it is proved whether or not we love and trust someone.

In a relationship, a woman's love is put on trial when a man seems to be low on cash. That is the best time to know if your fiancée can still love you; when the economy seems to be inflicting financial wounds on you! If the lady truthfully loves you, she will stay committed to you in any case.

In the same vein, God wants you to trust and believe in Him through all the varying circumstances of life. There is empirical medical proof that excessive worrying is detrimental to one's physical condition. Nervous tension, fretfulness and worry are known to trigger hypertension and eventually bring about cardiac complications. Learn to surrender all your burdens to Jesus and you will rest from your labors as He ministers solutions in your life.

"So, do not start worrying; "where will my food come from? Or my drink? Or my clothes? These are things the pagans are always concerned about. Your heavenly father in heaven knows that you need all these things."

(Mathew 6:31- 32)

It should excite you to know that God in heaven is fully aware that you need clothing, food and of course, to see your dream come true. He wants you to stop worrying about things tabulated above. He wants you to believe that He is more than able to meet all your needs.

Furthermore, you should not waste precious time worrying about material comforts of this world. Life is worth more than all these earthly things.

Sometimes people worry about not being abreast with clothing that is in vogue. Fashions come and fashions go, one musician has sung (Fred Sichilongo). Both Ladies and gentlemen; I know we love to be clad in designer apparel. Not that there is anything wrong or sinful about that obsession.

But the point is; set yourself free from cravings which are inconsequential when it comes to setting priorities in life. Seek first the Kingdom of God and all other things shall be added unto you. That is a powerful promise from God! God knows all your heart's desires. In His time, He makes everything beautiful.

"Don't worry about anything, but in all your prayers ask God for what you need, always asking him with a thankful heart."

(Philippians 4:6)

It is abundantly clear from this scripture that God does not want anyone to worry about anything. All one needs to do is to ask Him for that which is needed; in prayer and with a thankful heart. You could say, but I have a lot of problems. Your needs may be very numerous and varied. But that is not an issue with God. He is more than able to supply all your needs according to His riches in glory. Be compliant to the word of God and your way shall be made prosperous.

God cares for you

"It is God who clothes the wild grass-grass that today is here today and tomorrow, burnt up in the oven. Wont He be all the more sure to clothe you How little faith you have!"

(Mathew 6:30)

Even a cursory look at **Mathew 6:30** will motivate you to stop worrying about anything. It is God who clothes the grass! If He takes care of grass which is so short-lived what more you who he calls 'my child'? He definitely cares about your life and cherishes you more than the grass. You need to know that you are fearfully and wonderfully made in His image and likeness. You are special and no one can appreciate you more than God.

There is literally nothing God can fail to provide for you. The Bible clearly states that there is absolutely nothing too hard for God. Stop being a 'worrier' and become a prayer warrior! Ask God to reveal to you the strengths and gifts He has deposited into your life. With the skill set you have, God can guide you into doing something good for your generation. God created you for such a time like this. Though your dream/vision tarries, it shall surely come to pass. Use your challenges and bottlenecks as stepping stones for greater heights.

Worry has the potential to crowd out your God given dream. Fear not. Let no worry overtake your heart. Take stock of your life and figure out that which is causing you to distrust God. A number of people today are questioning God's goodness because all they see in their lives is trouble and stagnation. God is promising good things in their lives but the reality seems to be the contradictory.

Some people out of despondency are tempted to think that God only delivered and provided the older generation; the likes of Moses, Noah, and Elijah and so on and so forth. Little do they realize that God is the same yesterday, today and in perpetuity. He does not change. What He has done for others He can do for you. The trouble with people today is that they tend to go to God for help with a 'plan B' in place. God does not work like that. He who goes to God should believe in his heart that truly He is the rewarder of all those who diligently seek Him and that whatever is asked for in Jesus' name can be granted.

Do you know that there are people who 'believe' in God but are not expectant at all? There is a huge disparity between believing in God and expecting something from God. Many have just ended up believing that God cares for them without looking forward to anything from Him. This is the paradox that may be causing you to assume that God does not care about your wellbeing.

The Bible says even demons believe that God exists but that does not make them eligible to receive blessings from heaven. This reality check should make you understand that you really need to migrate from the level of just believing to the level of expectation. They say expectation is the mother of manifestation.

Worries can easily crowd out the love of God in your life. Worry can blind you to the reality of God's amazing grace. God has not brought you this far to let you down. He has preserved your life for a divine purpose. Cast all your cares onto the creator of the heaven and earth. Do not hold back any form of worry from Him. God does not just lighten your burden; He takes it away totally.

CHAPTER NINE
BE GRATEFUL

There is a way in which God rewards and blesses those with a grateful heart. God loves a grateful heart; a heart that says thanks even for a simple gift. Imagine you buy a present for your spouse and he/she receives it without showing any scintilla of gratitude. You will be filled with disappointment and frustration I guess. You will be left with no incentive to buy such a person another gift.

We are all obliged to have a thankful heart. Being grateful motivates the giver to continue being benevolent. Giving thanks is very important habit in our daily lives. Having a grateful heart attracts people that God has lined up in your life as conduits of his blessings.

Practice to say 'thank you' even to the most difficult superior at your place of work. That loud-mouthed manager who you shower with all sorts of unprintable invectives behind his/her back should alternatively be appreciated for many things.

The most critical dynamic is that he/she employed you and gives you a wage every month-end. Therefore, you should accord him/her absolute respect because through your boss God is providing for you. Furthermore, leadership comes from God. In this instance I am not referring to fake leadership but real leadership. Develop an attitude of thanking God for your leaders despite the consequences of their shortcomings. It doesn't matter what kind of treatment you receive from your superior. As a clear-headed child of God, learn to focus on the positive attributes of your overseer. Ill-treatment can be a positive learning curve. You are under such a boss for a divine reason. Look out for godly perspectives in every situation. Every cloud has a silver lining!

We are the way we are because we fail to appreciate the value of small things. I know for a fact that great things as a rule come in small packages; or in seed form to be metaphorical. Stop talking ill about your boss and work diligently as unto the Lord. Aim to impress your boss and let your hard work convict him/her of the dreadful attitude towards you.

If you want respect, give it to others. Your inhospitable boss is tutoring you on how to respect those in authority. You will appreciate that respect the day God will lift you to a position of authority. This is true if you dream of owning and running your own business one day. So, next time your boss shouts at you needlessly and unfairly, just smile at him or her. Show your boss that you are a person of integrity.

Here is a piece of advice. One-day surprise your boss by telling him/her how your welfare and that of the family has been enhanced because of the salary you get. Tell them that you are grateful and wish them God's blessings.

Your parents or guardians deserve special mention for making you who you are today. They deserve your unqualified support and respect for the sacrifices they made towards your personal interests. They may not have provided all your needs as you were growing up; but at least they put food on the table and paid for your education. All things considered, their contribution towards your childhood and education cannot and should never be disregarded.

Be appreciative that your parents chose between keeping your embryo and aborting it. A lot of God ordained lives have been callously terminated by mothers. Be thankful for having parents who chose to have you born and for their care and concern for your health.

Being grateful necessitates tracing your footprints back to your formative years. Only then will you see that you wouldn't have made it if it were not for your parents or guardians.

The truth about life is that we are what we are today because someone cared and gave us an opportunity to succeed. Your current social standing is courtesy of your parents or your custodians. Today you are sophisticated because someone paid your school fees. Chances are that you will never know how much your parents struggled and hustled to give you education. Surely you cannot afford to be ungrateful.

No man is self-made and no man is an island. Some people have been helped by their friends when no one else could. Have you taken time to appreciate that friend who bailed you out of a thorny situation? God impels you towards your destiny by connecting you to special people. Such networks are called destiny helpers

Personally, I have been facilitated by scores of people in my life's journey. I owe my current status to certain people whom God has placed in my life for a divine purpose. They are part of a matrix of factors that have propelled me to where I am now. I am forever grateful for their love and support in all my deeds.

Certain men and women have taught me life changing facts and without them I don't think I could have been here today. I remember in high school as a boarder, a man who worked in the school kitchen had a soft spot for me because according to him, I resembled his uncle. This man could give me extra food. He told me I could always go to him whenever I needed more food. I never understood his hospitality at that time and all I could tell him was 'thank you'.

My close friends also greatly benefited from the man's amazing goodwill. They could prevail on me to ask for more food even if I had enough. The gentleman's kindness was of enormous advantage to my three friends especially on days when beef or chicken were on the menu.

Now with the benefit of perception after the fact, there is no shadow of a doubt in my mind that it was God's will that I got attached to that man. Though my parents did provide my basic needs at boarding school, that man supplemented their efforts amazingly by giving me foodstuff. Because of him, I was adequately nourished. Don't you think that was God at work? There is no way a man, out of nothing, could act the way he did. Remember, God functions here on the earth through people. Take nothing for granted. God is always orchestrating and stage-managing things in ways we cannot not comprehend. Have a grateful heart even in little things.

Other people are not appreciative because the people who were meant to be their custodians disappointed them. Perhaps you were let down by people who were closest to you; relatives or friends. You may have been sexually abused by a close family member. Casting aside the bumpy side of life, there are people who have made us glad and pushed us to positions of importance.

If we focus on good experiences in life and overlook the disheartening ones, we shall develop a grateful heart. Satan would have remembered the bad times and act as if nothing good ever happened to us. Instead of keeping a record of wrongs, feed your mind with all the good experiences you have had. Being thankful is one of the greatest things you could ever do in life. If in the most unlikely event you have nothing to be grateful for, be grateful to God for the breath of life. Let everything that has breath praise the Lord.

There is always someone better than you.

The fact that you have an enviable job doesn't mean you are better than others. There is always someone better than you. If you think you are the best; think again! The thing is you have not yet met people who can make your achievements look below average. There is always someone a notch or two higher than you in whatever context. If you think it's your intelligence that made you land a managerial job, you are absolutely misguided.

It is just your time and be grateful for that. My point is to make you see the other side of a coin. The whole point is to make you realize that you owe what you have and are now, to someone who played a key role at some juncture and you have erased that one good deed from your remembrance!

Dear ladies,

How many adorable and educated young women are out there who are single? How many single and young mothers are struggling to raise just one child in your neighborhood? How many gorgeous and smart ladies desire to marry the type of man you are disrespecting and calling names? This barrage of questions should resonate with a number of ladies today. In case you are married, I want to feel you in on the fact that many ladies are seeking what you already have and they are willing to do everything possible to have what you have but don't appreciate it. I guess you know what I am trying to affirm here.

That husband you call 'not man enough' is trying his best to ward off advances from single beautiful ladies because he still loves you. In spite of your apparent lack of affection for him, he is still committed to you. Begin to appreciate him because you only know the value of what you have when you have lost it.

My simple advice for you is; appreciate our spouse before your next-door neighbor seduces him. Be wise and be grateful. Stop thinking your spouse does not deserve you because of your beauty. Marriage is not about beauty. It transcends that threshold of thinking! If it were all about your body and shape, don't you think your man could have moved away from you a long time ago; for someone more eye-catching and seductive than you?

Be there for him and ensure he feels appreciated as your man before your relationship depreciates. Ensure that you lend him your support in all his endeavors. Let him know that he is a faithful man who tries pretty hard to play his role as the head of the home.

There is a tendency I detest intensely. It is the tendency of appreciating people after they have passed away. We eulogize people at their memorial service but never say anything praiseworthy when they are alive. This is an exceedingly diabolical tendency. It is good to make people aware that they are appreciated. *Theroux writes,* "One of the commodities in life that most people can't get enough of is compliments. The ego is never so intact that one can't find a hole in which to plug a little praise. Compliments by their nature are decidedly bio-gradable and tend to dissolve hours or days after we receive them-which is why we can always use another."

CHAPTER TEN
DEFY THE SYSTEM

The way we think and make choices is by and large influenced by the values and belief systems accepted by the environment we live in. It is the existent belief systems that have a bearing on our culture and mores. If the belief systems are based on detrimental values, they should be challenged by any person wanting to go ahead in life. Yes! You can be the change agent for the paradigm to shift.

Our values and belief systems are the undercurrents that control the general behavior of any given society. Issues of corruption, bribery, prostitution, theft embedded in our cultural values must be defied because they are inimical to the will of God.

There are many undercurrents that deter us from making it in life. There are some families where it is unheard of to be a university graduate. Yet in other families even possessing a bicycle is a far cry. I am sure what I have alluded to does ring a bell; it sounds familiar. Somebody in the blood line of your family must defy this poverty mentality, and that person is you. You can redeem your family from a generational succession of mediocrity. The sight of your relative's rustic behavior, poverty, and illiteracy should spur you to change the story of your family!

A story is told about how a certain young man refused to go to university on the premise that he was well connected to influential people who could finance his everyday life. According to him, he had connections with people holding important public offices. To him money was not an issue because the connections were involved in clandestine but money-spinning business deals. If he needed money a mere phone call was enough.

This young man has his priorities upside down. Living on money suspected to be proceeds of crime puts his life at risk. He should have opted to get educated and find himself a well-paid job. We all know that crime does not pay; it does not secure your future at all.

The truth of the matter is that his future hangs in the balance. He is living on borrowed time. His frame of mind is constructed by the undercurrent of corruption. He is born in a society that thinks corruption is the way to go. This is an example of a systemic offense that is no longer viewed as a vice.

Every problem has got a solution and every disease or condition has a remedy. Your influence could make the desired change in your community. Issues of corruption, bribery, prostitution, theft and defilement exist because of a paradigm that has habituated our morals and values.

I have seen a scenario where a person jumps a queue and offers a bribe so that he can be served ahead of other people in that queue. The service provider also accepts the bribe. Corruption is a system that defines what kind of a community we are. We believe in cutting corners and bribing our way into positions of advantage at the detriment of other people's opportunities.

God may give an assignment that requires uprooting deep-seated negative value systems. Do not be afraid to challenge the status quo and make a difference. Christians are born to make a difference and be the difference in your generation.

As an individual you may be abetting some evil systems in your environment. You may intentionally or inadvertently be promoting undercurrents that hamper social and economic development. We are either promoting or participating in retrogressive systems that take the country backwards.

As a child of God, you must separate yourself from aberrant behavior and become an advocate of good morals and good citizenship.

There is definitely something you can do about some traditions that you feel should not be there in the first place. Things like sexual cleansing of widows and defiling under aged girls as rituals in the name of tradition must not be tolerated in this day and age.

We are all alive to the existence of these wicked and outdated belief systems. It is incumbent upon Christians to sanitize societal life with the gospel of Jesus Christ. The need to evangelize has never been greater than now; when what were once vices are now enshrined in the UN charter as human rights. In view of the aforesaid, ensure that you are among the drivers of positive change even at household and community level. Strive to be the change you want to see, even as you wish and hope for a brighter and successful future for all.

CHAPTER ELEVEN
ROAR FOR A GOOD CAUSE

What are you irritable about? Are you really sure you have to complain and blame others for what you are going through? What makes you think the way you think with regard to the alarming levels of poverty and the high cost of living? What are you doing about the problems your country is facing? Are you part of the solution or part of the problem? What are you doing about the many challenges that your neighborhood is facing today? Let's attempt to answer this 'questionnaire' with all sincerity.

In the times we are living in, people have gone into grievance mode. People are so apprehensive and worked up with regard the economic and political state of affairs in the country. Admittedly, things are not looking good on many fronts! Virtually everyone has one grievance all the other. Some people are complaining about everything. They simply say everything is bad and the country is on its knees. Well, assuming our leaders have made off beam political and economic choices which have brought us where we are, what is the way forward? Two wrongs do not make a right. Of course, the finger of indictment is pointing at the authorities but what is our role in resolving the economic gridlock, should be our question.

Regardless of which side of the political divide you belong to, come let us reason together with the hope of taking our nation forward in spite of its multidimensional issues.

It is your unassailable right to express your views on matters concerning your welfare. You are absolutely entitled to your opinion; and incidentally, your opinion should be appreciated. But the blame game will not bring about the development we desire to see. What are you doing about the things you are not happy about?

To add a new angle to our discourse, to a certain degree we are in economic dire straits because of some ill-informed decisions we make every day in our lives. Some people try to save face by blaming the economy when in fact the economy has little to do with their vulnerability. Government is a sounding board for our own inefficiencies and inconsistency.

Poor individual decisions and choices will never earn you a good life. Before you think of apportioning blame on others, take stock of your personal decisions. This is a sobering reality check and an audit of your decision-making aptitude. Ask yourself how you got where you are and find out if external forces had anything to do with your tight spot. These are questions you need to answer yourself.

You are responsible for your own life, and real or perceived failures by government are a mere scapegoat. The fact that other people are making it in the same economy should be an eye opener for you.

If you were the president of your country today, do you think every citizen including your relatives would love and support you? By the way, how are you managing your relationships? How is your home being managed? I have seen people complain and lobby for change of leadership because, they believe those in leadership are incompetent and not delivering on their promises.

 My question is, if you can't administer your small family, are you any better than those you are criticizing and refusing to appreciate? Before you remove the speck in your friends' eye, remove the log from yours first.

Look to God and not the government. Those who put their confidence in God will never be disappointed. Governments, especially African governments, do not owe you a living. The government and the world are both impersonal entities. Only God is personal. He deals with us at a personal level. If you do not fall back on this truth, you will live a life of criticism in perpetuity.

 Stand up and do something with your life. Wake up from your comfort zone. While you are belligerent and crying foul, others are making measurable progress in their business ventures. While you are finger pointing, someone is negotiating a deal worth millions of dollars. While you are wasting your time playing the blame game and cursing, your workmate is being promoted for being resourceful.

No government will ever meet all your needs. The promises they make are never fulfilled in totality. But the government of heaven whose economy never suffers a slump or downward spiral should be your dependable and unfaltering supplier of all your needs. Put your trust in the Lord and your heart will not be troubled.

CHAPTER TWELVE
COMMIT YOURSELF TODAY

"To everything there is a season, and a time to every purpose under the heaven. A time to be born, and a time to die; a time to plant, and a time to pluck up that which was planted."

(Ecclesiastes 3:1-2)

In life you must have the anointing of the sons of Issachar who were good at reading times and seasons. It is always imperative to discern what time it is and be able to do what needs to be done in each day rather than deferring today's tasks to a later date. Theorists have said something to the effect that procrastination is the thief of time.

The Bible makes it crystal clear that there is a season and a time to every purpose under the sun. Everyone has an assignment to carry out here on earth while it is still called day! It is pivotal to be in sync with God's timing so that you do not miss that critical intersection between time and opportunity.

Every one of us has been given time as a precious gift. Timeliness is what matters in delivering something. Always remember that time lost can never be recovered. While you are dithering and vacillating time is on the move! Avoid moving with the hand brake on. God works with times and seasons. Be spiritually on cue!

God gives each one of us twenty-four hours a day, no more no less. What differentiates winners and losers is how the time is utilized by both parties. It simply means God is so impartial that He has equally distributed the resource of time to all and sundry. It is therefore important to exploit each day towards adding value to your life and to your entire generation. I cannot overstate the fact that God has exceptional and definite plans for your life. He has plans to prosper you, giving you hope and an expected end.

 Unless you come to this realization and commit yourself today, you cannot accomplish much here on earth. I entreat you to rise to the occasion and take God's plans for you in your stride. Embrace the will of God with all that is within you!

"I returned, and saw under the sun, that the race is not to the swift, nor the battle to the strong, neither yet bread to the wise, nor yet riches to men of understanding, nor favor to men of skill; but time and chance happeneth to them all."

(Ecclesiastes9:11)

No one can repudiate the truth that time and chance is singularly and severally given to all. There is a sense and context in which the playing field has been leveled by God. But what you do with your time and opportunities makes a world of a difference.

Some people invest their money in a viable business ventures while others spend theirs irresponsibly: at the same and in similar circumstances. In the fullness of time the outcomes will show who made a wise decision and who did not.

If you are a student already or you are preparing to enroll in one, take education seriously because it is an investment that may determine your future social and economic status. Time is very vital resource to man and should therefore be managed with due diligence.

The same applies to companies. Discreet time management is what brings about new opportunities and new clients. Therefore, train your employees to be wary about time. Clients do not take kindly to any degree of time wasting. They have busy schedules just like you. As a company, one of the things that will distinguish you from the rest is how you manage your time.

It is consequently shrewd to make the most of every available opportunity because you never know what developments it may bring into your life. In addition, even to the supposed unqualified people, time and chance is given. This just goes to demonstrate how equitable and considerate our God is. The people that we label as the disadvantaged or vulnerable were not born in impoverished families by choice. It is just by the accident of nature that they find themselves on the undesirable side of earthly financial systems.

The fact is God does not consult your past or your social background to determine your future. God stirs the gift and talents inherent in you to usher you into the desired future. Hence you need to be spiritually alert and sensitive so you may discern where the Lord is leading you. Make every effort to do what you are good at and God will impel you to your predestined position.

Look at some of the most illustrious footballers that are on our lips nearly every day. Most of them have very humble education or no formal education at all. Yet their football flair has ushered them onto the world stage. They are taking home incredible sums of cash every week. They are more affluent than university dons and other well-read people. The secret behind their success is that they discovered their God given art, harnessed it to perfection and the rest is history. They realized through football that they were born with a silver spoon in their mouths. Success is your portion if you are tranquil enough to detect your bequest and run with it. If they did it without education then, you can do it also.

"But the day of the Lord will come as a thief. On that day the heavens will disappear with a shrill noise, the heavenly bodies will burn up and be destroyed, and the earth with everything in it will vanish."

(2 peter3:10)

In all probability you know and have heard that one day heaven and earth shall pass away. In case you have not been aware of this imminent event, now you have been informed. Now that you know this future event, will you stand akimbo and do nothing about your dream?

It is a matter of urgency that you begin to live your life as the Lord has mapped it. Your congenital skill set is intended to be the key to unbolt your veiled destiny. When will you prove to the community that ***you have what it takes*** to be a good singer, an accountant or entrepreneur? It is an embarrassment to the

Lord for you to die with unexploited potential. You must die empty!

The sobering reality is that once you give up the ghost, you can no longer use your gifting. Dreams are only feasible, attainable and functional whilst you are still alive here on earth. The time to arise and shine above mediocrity is now. Stop thinking there is still time. Now is the time for self-actualization. Do not allow opportunity after opportunity to fly past. Seize the opportunity and the moment!! Your destiny is awaiting your magnificent arrival.

"I have done my best in the race, I have run the full distance, and I have kept the faith. And now the prize of victory is waiting for me... "

(2 Timothy 4:7)

Every one of us has a specific race to run. For this reason, do not try to run someone else's race. Find your own track or lane and compete with yourself. Fulfillment is only probable the instant you discover your mission and passion in life. You were born to be a gift to your family and to society at large by doing what only you were configured by God to do. Moreover, life is meant to be lived and enjoyed with the consciousness that one day we will give an account with regard to how we handled our individual talents. The earlier you discover your inborn skill set the better. That is how you avoid trial and error. You will be doing things in a clued-up approach and with clockwork precision.

There is always a profit for whatever work you do for the Kingdom of God. It may be to comfort or edify someone. Hence strive to do your spiritual chores with gladness and to the best of your ability; with the knowledge that you are advancing kingdom purposes. It pays to know that your labor in the Lord is not in vain. Keep away from giving lame pretexts for failing to do what you are mandated, empowered and equipped by God to do. There are things which only you can do; thus, the act of withholding your effort is a contradiction in terms.

One of the worst things in life is that defining moment when you begin to rue the opportunities you missed to do certain things when you were a certain age. You look back lamentably and with hindsight; and wish you could have done things differently.

 This brings me to the chronicle of King Saul in *1 Samuel15*. There was a time when Saul was told to carry out an operation with detailed directives from God. As fate would have it, Saul for some strange reason went against the instructions on how to conduct the operation. Because he openly flouted God's statutes the operation did not go well and Saul became a miserable figure from then on.

The Bible says to obey is better than to sacrifice. Here is a test for you. Look for people you should have obeyed and did not and ask for forgiveness. Tell them they were right then and still right now! Don't feel timid or be daunted by pride or fear of shame. It is for your own good and benefit.

Now that you know what is expected of you, there should be
no more time wasting. Stand up and be counted. Get
up and prepare to leave your foot prints in the sands of
history.

There should be no shadow of a doubt in your mind that you
do have what it takes to do exploits for God. God's abilities are
at work in you by His word. Be courageous to do things which
others have failed to do. Let the history books write your name
among the heroes of the faith. Be a history maker for Jesus!
Come out from the comfort zone and take up the challenge.

CHAPTER THIRTEEN
STICK TO YOUR PURPOSE

"To be yourself in a world that is constantly trying to make you something else is the greatest accomplishment."

Ralph Waldo Emerson

Twins are born from the same mother and father and relatively at the same time. However, in spite of having comparable particulars, their thinking processes are not the same. As a matter of fact, it can be postulated that they do not have the same fate. This should be a point of departure to start thinking realistically different concerning your existence here on earth.

Everyone is born for a specific purpose. For that reason, living a purpose-driven life is what gives paternity to a quality of life that is epitomized by happiness, contentment, fulfillment and evident self-actualization. Trying to 'copy and paste' the life-style of your next-door neighbor may be a costly mistake. This is because we all have divergent destinies and hence different personal details. The purposes God would want to be fulfilled through people vary from person to person.

The citation from Ralph Waldo Emerson is encouraging you to stick to your God ordained job description in a world that is constantly trying to make you something else. Emerson is basically saying that staying focused in the midst of contrary voices is the greatest accomplishment. If you agree with his sentiments, do your best and practice them by sticking to your purpose and God will do the rest for you.

With so much happening around the globe, everyone wants to be celebrated. To have ambitions of success is not an offence by all accounts. But it becomes wrong when you try to copy and live someone else's life. It is an affront to God's will when you think His configuration of your life is inferior to that of others'. In fact, the most horrible thing you can ever do is to stop living your life as designed by God because of being converted by other people's conditions.

It has been established that people who try to be what they are not always land in deep trouble. They violate both legal and spiritual limits in order to measure up with the people they admire or covet. Some even go to the extent of making very risky financial decisions like getting huge loans that they cannot even properly service. Some end up losing whatever they staked as collateral. Trying to be what God never intended for you to be is indeed a recipe for disaster in your life. Never temper with your identity and God's parameters for your life.

The problem with some people is that they always want to be everywhere and please everybody. They pay no attention to who they are and where they ought to be and what they ought to be doing! Being a people pleaser is a very difficult job. It is unfeasible to gratify everybody all the time. If the same world looked at Jesus with mixed feelings in spite of the many signs and wonders He performed, how about you and I who claim to be following the footsteps of Jesus Christ? Do yourself a favor by seeking a revelation of your assignment here on earth.

"Then Saul said to Samuel, 'I have sinned. I have violated the Lords command and your instructions. I was afraid of the men and so I gave in to them."

(1 Samuel 15:24)

Being a people pleaser does not earn you any favor from both God and the people you are striving to please. Seeking the approval of men is typically inimical to God's will for your life. The gist of the story in the scripture in question is that Saul was the right choice to rule over Israel when Israel demanded to have king like other nations did.

During his reign, Saul was so mindful of people and had the knack to please them. As a result of being a people pleaser, Saul disobeyed God Almighty who had made him the first king of Israel. Saul decided to please man instead of observing God's rules and regulations.

The fact that Saul was a people pleaser cannot be in dispute. You cannot fault anyone for assuming that Saul cared less about the will of God over his life. He took the expedient course by respecting man while overlooking the reality that everyone here on earth has got a different destiny. Remember we started this chapter by asserting that even twins may have dissimilar purposes for their lives. The fact that your closest friend is a pastor does not suggest you too should become a man of the cloth! If God has shown you the way to your destiny, you can never lose your bearings.

In the grand scheme of things, everyone is entitled to their opinion. If you try to please everyone in life you will never be happy yourself at all. To be more brutal, let me say you will never get to live your intended life. I wish I could find the most compelling approach of saying how ineffectual it is to make everyone happy around you. Every normal person can relate to the allegation that people are very difficult to please.

The foregoing sentiments should make you understand that you are not them and they are not you. Get understanding and pull yourself together. Focus your energies on being what God created you to be and in your daily grind you will be pleasing God. Saul's account should stimulate you to comply with God's divine bidding. Avoid trying to fit into other people's visions and missions for the sole purpose of being accepted.

For this reason, it is of enormous spiritual implication to discern what you were born for. I can assure you that once you know what you were born for; your life will be a statement of godliness with contentment.

Nobody here on earth can make you and grow you into what you ought to be. It is only God who clothes the grass of the field and feeds the birds of the air and not man. If you agree with me, make every effort to become what God wants you to be and He will supply all the logistics you need until your journey's end. He will equip you according to the demands of your journey. The Bible says cursed is he who puts his trust in the arm of flesh. Trust God and not man.

As you believe God for a brighter future, ensure that all that is required of you is done accordingly and God will reward your works. For everyone reaps what they sow

You have been blessed with life today and it is incumbent upon you to make something of your life. Since life is lived one day at a time, be diligent with each day and the happenings therein. Be a person that is preoccupied with seeing God's purposes here on earth being actualized.

Refuse to be a people pleaser for it is a costly and futile exercise. In God's economy, people pleasers always draw a blank. In other words, they live on borrowed lifestyles and therefore they lack that essential element called fulfillment. Even if they know that something is amiss, they will be quiet about it.

Did you know that there is always someone better than you? It sounds so crazy but it is true. Consider the scripture below and thank God because He wants you, and nobody else to do what you are doing.

"Samuel said to him, 'the lord has torn the kingdom of Israel from you today and has given it to one of your neighbors-to one better than you."

(1 Samuel15:28)

If by any chance you have never believed that there was always someone better than you, it's time for you to accept that you have been mistaken all the while. The fact that you hold a certain position does not mean there is no person who can perform better than you. There is always someone better and more competent than you.

Consequently, be very careful about your performance even where careers are concerned. Be competent and sensitive enough in your day to today duties. Do your job to the best of your ability. In fact, do your work as unto the Lord. Let your superiors know that you can carry out your duties with conscientiousness and loyalty.

Furthermore, maintain your integrity and moral propriety when workmates try to lure you into secret romantic relationships. Do not let your feelings ride roughshod over your better judgment. Do not fall into that temptation because the spiritual stakes are very high.

If you are a lady, do not indulge in carnal knowledge with your so called boyfriend who claims to love you. There is always someone better than him who is willing to wait for you until you are ready for it in godly setting; that is marriage. Ladies must learn to cherish the sanctity of their bodies and say no to illicit sex. Hold your morals close to your chest!

Society desires to see genuine girl power and not what is obtaining in this day and age. We are weary of seeing girls flaunting themselves like articles of trade through lewd exposure and scanty dressing. When you 'advertise' yourself, for sure men will come and buy your body and damp you after using you. Real men are looking for real women to spend their lifetimes with.

It is of the essence for Christian girls to prove to the world that they are cut from a different fabric. A Christian girl does not dress like worldly girls do. Make a difference and you will not be a victim of vultures. By vultures I mean men who are bent on using you for sex but discern you are not marriage substance. When they feel like marrying, they find themselves a decent wife from the village. So, if I were you I would be very cautious and make sure that I dress in a decent manner and to the glory of God.

"The will to win, the desire to succeed, the urge to reach your full potential... these are the keys that will unlock the door to personal excellence"

Confucius

As you endeavor to reach the zenith of your life, maintain a positive mindset to the effect that nothing is impossible. Believe in yourself and trust God even as you ensure that His purpose for your life here on earth is being fulfilled.

CHAPTER FOURTEEN
REMAIN IN YOUR TIME ZONE

Both the sun and the moon are essential as far the operations of the galaxy are concerned. They give light and shine when at the right time. The sun shines during the day and the moon during the night. The sun's purpose is to give light during the day and the moon has got no qualms with that because it has the whole night to itself. Don't compare the moon to the sun because they both shine in their due time. You can only compare two things of the same magnitude.

God makes everything beautiful in its time. Time is an opportunity to do things right and differently. Time is a gift to prove ourselves. In fact, time is everything you need to be what you have always wanted to be.

In the Bible, Cain and Abel were blessed and gifted differently. Both Cain and Abel were farmers. Cain's mainstay was tilling the land while Abel his younger brother specialized in animal husbandry. When time and opportunity were given to both to give a sacrifice to the Lord; we see how God reacted to both individuals. God in His wisdom accepted Abel's offering and on the other hand rejected Cain's.

God's rejection of Cain's sacrifice fomented antipathy and bad blood between him and his brother Abel. Cain's intense hatred for his brother led him into slaying him in cold blood. Both parties had an opportunity to do what was right in the sight of God. Both had the choice and will to give the sacrifice to the best of their ability and capacity. Abel made the right sacrifice while Cain disregarded the protocols and conventions that regulated the process of sacrificing.

Why did Cain kill his brother? The hypothetical answer is that Cain must have felt that it was his brother's fault that God had rejected him and his offering. In other words, he started comparing himself to his brother. The problem is not those we envy. The problem is with you and me for developing envy and hatred for those who are meticulous in doing what God bids them to do. The problem is with you for not doing the right thing when you had the opportunity and choice to do so. A typical failure in life is someone who envies and talks ill about successful people. The rich have been called names for being rich and the poor have not been spared for being poor as well.

Thought

Many occurrences including murder could be prevented if we all realized, accepted and remained in our particular time zones. The truth about life is that the poor will always be there, but it doesn't have to be you. People who choose to ignore the truth and the underlying principles for wealth creation will invariably spite those who thrive, and inevitably charge the government for their lack of advancement.

What people do when money passes through their hands is left to conjecture. A survey should be conducted to ascertain what individuals do with their salary or wage. Do they spend or invest it? Generally speaking, people are where they are because of the choices they made at decisive intersections of their lives. When you find yourself at crossroads it is prudent to choose the right road.

As already said, time is an opportunity to do what is right and what is right is for you to be yourself and remain in your time zone. Remain in your time zone doing what is right. Before your time comes, ensure that you prepare adequately in order to possess and sustain that which you are hoping for in life.

 There are people who desire to become CEOs but they are doing nothing about their educational qualifications. They are seated shouting 'I receive' as if success comes that easily! God expects you to be very patient and doing something worthwhile as you wait for your time and season. With God's help, work yourself up to the top.

Envy and jealous is a lethal recipe that can spell your fall from grace. The moment you sense that you are envying other people, take curative steps to avert that negative energy. Some people kill not because they are professional killers but they are prodded by unbridled envy and jealousy.

Be grateful to God for what you have currently. Count your blessing, naming them one by one. It will surprise you what the Lord had done for you. Be content and take hold of the opportunities that come your way. Don't allow yourself to be led astray by jealousy. Ensure that you rule over it before it rules over you. Witchcraft is a synonym of covetousness and jealousy.

Acknowledge and celebrate those who are on cloud nine now knowing that your time is just around the corner. Ensure that covetousness does not shortchange your joy and contentment. Life is too short for envy and jealous to feel your senses. Bear in mind, in God's economy the race is neither for the swift nor the wise but time and chance is given to them all.

The way forward

God lifts the humble and resists the proud. In His own time, God will bless you with what is befitting for your life. God does not withhold any good thing from His own. If He withholds something from you; it means it is not good or not meant for you. Remember, God knows the end from the beginning and He knows what you need. The God who resists the proud is the same God who lifts the humble.

Don't treat people based on your past

Don't bring your past into current issues except if you want to draw lessons from there retrospectively. Otherwise, it is dangerous to deal with current affairs based on your past experiences. Doing so may result in loss of opportunities. There people who have spurned potential husbands or wives because of being afraid that disappointments and hurts of past relationships may repeat themselves.

Forestalling of being hurt again is logical but do not be too mindful of the past to the extent of missing a golden opportunity in whatever context. Operating under the specter of long-gone horrible experiences should not take priority over your better judgment. The past should have no consequential influence over your present and future because it is already gone. If you were rich yesterday and today you happen to be poor, people will look at you based on your current status. You have nothing accept your new curriculum vitae. No one cares about your past glory. People will relate to you based on your current and prevailing status.

Don't relate to people using the residue of the venom from your past hurts and emotional wounds. How on earth can you explain how you have managed to store bitterness for a person who grieved you forty years ago? Before you lose business opportunities and business partnerships, learn to separate your past from your present and future to come.

As a matter of fact, forget the former things and embrace the present and the future. It's not fair for you to treat others based on your past. It is stupidity to dwell in the past. Metaphorically speaking, take a personal exodus from genesis to revelation. I know men and women who have died as bachelors and spinsters just because of one painful broken relationship. They declared that all men or women are bad people.

I know a young lady who missed a great man because she made a doctrine out of her nasty experience with one or two men. The doctrine says 'all men are not trustworthy'. Today the lady is going out with any man who manifests interest in marrying her. Her looks are no longer the same. She is no longer marketable, to use business lingo. I always get emotional whenever I hear her lament and rue the last missed opportunity. The past has passed. Relocate yourself from the past to the present. Throw away the lenses that make you magnify the past. Break the rear-view mirror and watch the screen in front of you. Life is a forward motion!

Do what is right

God is the self-existent one. From beginning to the end, He is God and you are part of His creation. Everything you see was constituted by the creative word of God. God is the same yesterday, today and forevermore. He never changes and nothing can ever alter His narrative and specifics.

God doesn't have a problem. Man does not only have problems; he is a problem. Some of the things you want in this life have no value adding properties. God knows exactly what you need in your life. God knows the precise provisions you need at every phase of your life. God is and Has everything you need in all your earthly activities. Fix your mind on God's agenda and He will take care of your personal agenda. Let uprightness reign supreme in your life and God will cheerfully bequeath you with unspeakable blessings.

As earlier mentioned, it is man who has problems and not God. Therefore, this fact calls for each one of us to think what God could possibly need. Remember, the earth is the Lord's and everything therein. As such, you are required to go into business with God. In other words, you must at all costs align yourself to God who owns the very things you want and need.

Nobody wants to go into partnership with someone who is not proficient enough. If you desire to do business in collaboration with somebody, ensure that the person has the acumen needed in accomplishing the common goal you are pursuing.

God is the custodian of all secrets to success. He is the one who teaches us how to create wealth. He is the best business partner and consultant since He knows the earth and all its resources more than any other person. He created the earth and all the natural resources making Him the most well-informed business partner you can ever dream of.

Stop the excuse game

'God's time is the best' has been used by a cross section of people as a pretext for procrastination. It is said there is always a good reason and the real reason! Some people claim that they are where they are because God's time has not yet come for them to prosper. They give all sorts of excuses just to make themselves feel good and reassured.

 But is never the whole truth in most cases. Many people fail to take advantage of the environment they are in. The issue is not that God's appointed moment has not yet come. The problem is that people have mistaken 'God's timing' with their failure to distinguish God's method of doing things. Many have despised small beginnings. A lot of people fail to see a real business opportunity because its magnitude is not what they are expecting from God. Some good things in life come in small packages. They come in seed form!

Procrastination on the other hand, is another big issue which requires so much energy to get rid of. To procrastinate is to put things on hold thinking you still have more time in your life. In other words, to procrastinate is to fail to do things at a given time without having proper reasons. In order to make progress in life, one must ensure that they do things in a timely manner.

There are things we must do today because tomorrow may not be conducive. Today's chores are not meant to be done tomorrow.

Develop a heart that always wants to fulfill what each day demands. Lethargy, slothfulness and procrastination can wrongly be ascribed to God's time being still in the offing. Seek God's perspectives for a particular day; after all we live one at a time. Defy procrastination it is a thief of time. Treat every day as a small step towards realizing your set goals. Avoid a situation where you are compelled to start working under pressure because time is running out. Time is a resource that must be used wisely and optimally.

Stop saying God's time is the best when you are doing nothing with your life. Age may be catching up with you and soon you may not have the time and the energy to achieve anything tangible. Your age mates may have made notable advancements. Some are married and others own businesses just to show you that time is not your best ally. In fact, we are all encouraged to 'redeem the time because days are evil.' Things have changed and the clock keeps on ticking.

Yesterday is gone and today will go. Yesterday is history and you have today to revise your ways. While it is factual that God's time is the best, it is equally important to be doing something constructive during the waiting window period. Waiting does not imply the folding your arms. God is known for blessing the work of people's hands. God's time must find your hands on the deck.

Defend the defenseless

Being rich is a blessing but if your money causes you to look down upon others that is a big concern. In as much as there are rich people, there are also the underprivileged and the uneducated. The uneducated are oblivious to their human rights and their ignorance allows people to take advantage of them. Some people have lost their hard-earned properties because they could not defend themselves from the rich and powerful in society. The truth is that some people use their money and influence to intimidate and humiliate the vulnerable. Some people have lost millions in straight forward law suits simply because they could not afford to hire a lawyer.

Allow me to make a sweeping statement: we all want to be rich and wealthy. In the likely event that we become rich, we must ask ourselves key questions. You must put a finger on the reason why God has allowed you to create wealth. Being prosperous is not a problem; the problem is why do you want to be rich?

When success gets to someone's head, they begin to do strange and unpalatable things. They begin to treat the poor as if the poor are the dregs of society. They begin to live extravagant lifestyles and ignore the plight of the poor. The essence of God giving us the power to create wealth is that once we prosper we must become a blessing to others. God blesses people through people. If you don't keep this principle in your frame of mind, wealth will begin to control you.

 As you make money and become powerful in society, ensure that you do what is right with your power and money. Don't abuse your influence to suppress others. Remain humble and sober when God in His time lifts you. Be a blessing and not a curse to the downtrodden in society. Be their solution and not their problem.

CHAPTER FIFTEEN
THE IMPORTANCE OF CHARACTER

A good name is better than a fine smelling perfume. Companies spend so much money in creating a brand that represents their corporate image by way of advertisement, and other means of marketing their corporation. Those of you coming from the business and marketing background may know what I am talking about. A brand is like the personality or face of an organization. In business it is called a trademark. A company has a character so to speak.

Personality can be delineated as the combination of characteristics or qualities that form an individual's distinctive character. Its synonyms are character, nature, disposition, temperament, make-up, persona, psych or identity. Therefore, Personality is that which differentiates you from others.

Personality can further be defined as the characteristic set of behaviors, cognitions and emotional patterns that evolve from biological and environmental factors. Trait-based personality theories describe personality as the traits that guess a person's conduct. Therefore, it is very essential to make certain that your personality or character is underpinned by honesty and decorum. Make certain that you brand yourself as a praiseworthy person who people can do business with.

A person's life is not defined by the possessions he owns. It is defined by what is left of him when his earthly possessions are subtracted from his person. The bottom line is that a person is defined by his personality. In simple language, life is defined by what you are as a person. The way you think and make decisions and the way you behave and respond to various circumstances.

Many people today especially the youth have set their sights on material things. Once again let me state that there is nothing wrong with accruing material things. My concern is if your character is not stable, prosperity might take you away from God.

If you have a weak character you will fail to handle success. Instead success will handle you. It is extremely disheartening to see the young people giving up on their dreams all because of hankering to have fast money. If it is ladies, they may engage themselves in prostitution in order to make easy money. With the gifting you have coupled with your uniqueness, you can make it without cutting corners.

God stands ready to ensure you succeed in life. Work on your character and tap into your unique skill set for inclusive personal development. Ask God to strengthen your character so that when prosperity comes you will not depart from His law. Ensure that your soul or the inner man prospers spiritually. That way everything else will fall into place. There is no true success before the soul prospers.

CHAPTER SIXTEEN
YOUR OTHER SIDE

"Jesus said unto him, if thou canst believe, all things are possible to him that believeth."

(Mark 9:23)

Man is a tripartite being compromising the body, soul and spirit. The real man is the spirit who dwells in the body. (**2 Corinthians 5:1-3**).Man believes with the spirit which is metaphorically called the heart. (Romans 10:10). With his spirit, man is able to believe. The world says seeing is believing but in the things of God believing is seeing. For believers do not walk by sight but by faith. The Bible says to him that believes, all things shall be possible.

Jesus said unless you are born again you cannot see the Kingdom of God. In other words, for you to receive the kingdom of God in your heart you ought to believe in Jesus Christ and that He rose from the dead. You must confess that He is Lord over your life. When that happens, you are never the same again. You are now a new creation; the old self has passed away and behold the new you have come forth.

It is no longer you that is living but Christ living in you. Your spirit and His Spirit are now able to have sweet spiritual union. You have been regenerated and impacted with the nature and life of Christ. You are born again! You now have the mind of God because you have received divine ability and supernatural wisdom. Your life is no longer inhibited by limitations.

Whatever your background is and whatever your current socioeconomic status may be, change can take effect in your life if you are willing and obedient. The secret is to have your spirit regenerated. Your spirit is the candle of the Lord and the Lord guides you through it *(Proverbs 20:27).*

The spirit of man is the candle of the Lord. It searches even the innermost recesses of a man. The Bible says from your heart (spirit) emanate all issues of life. This spell out why the Bible commands believers to guard their hearts. The heart is the wellspring of life. (Proverb 4:23) "Keep thy heart with all diligence; for out of it are the issues of life."

Building up your Spirit for success

The real you is your spirit, commonly known as the inner man. Since all elements of life originate from your spirit, it means the seeds of success are entrenched in your spirit. That's why God prioritizes the building up of your spirit for success.

"And now, brethren, I commend you to God, and to the word of his grace, which is able to build you up, and to give you an inheritance among all them which are sanctified."

(Acts 20:32)

The word of God is the only certified material to be used in building your life. God uses His word to build lives. The man you are destined you to be, your expected future status is all factored in the word. Whenever God wants to deposit something in your spirit He invariably uses His word. There are moments when the written word (logos) becomes a personal word (rhema). The word becomes flesh in your life. The word somewhat activates your hidden potential. The word is prophetic by nature.

As your intake of the word increases exponentially, you are essentially bracing yourself for success. You are encoding your mind for success. As you feed your mind with the word of God, the potential in you begins to find expression. The word of God primes you for eventual excellence and greatness.

 When you get born again, you are ushered into a life of endless possibilities. You begin to live a life of unspeakable advantage.

Using the word of God

"This book of the law shall not depart out of thy mouth; but thou shalt meditate therein day and night, that thou mayest observe to do according to all that is written therein: for then thou shalt make thy way prosperous, and then thou shalt have good success."

(Josh 1:8)

Hearing and reading the word of God alone is not the end of the story. You must go a step further by applying it, put it to work, try it out! This is where the issue of meditation comes in.

To meditate on the word of God means to 'ponder, to think through, to mutter, to speak and roar' the word of God. In meditation you are consciously and purposely thinking through the word, muttering it through self-talk. As you speak forth to yourself, you are actually programming your spirit and mind for success and prosperity. The scripture above shows that meditation on the word will enable you to observe and obey it so as to make your way prosperous and have good success.

Speaking in tongues

"But ye, beloved, building up yourselves on your most holy faith, praying in the Holy Ghost."

(Jude 1:20)

Praying in the Holy Ghost is praying in tongues. Speaking in tongue builds you up and strengthens you for life. Praying in tongues builds your spirit and your faith. You become more responsive to the leading and guidance of the Holy Spirit as you speak in tongues more regularly. Speaking in tongues and speaking the word of God builds you up into an edifice.

There is the other side of you, you can do anything and reach to the highest peak of your success.

CHAPTER SEVENTEEN
USE YOUR TONGUE WELL–
SPEAK POSITIVELY

Everyone can relate to the fact that words have a lot of creative power. The Bible says the power of life and death lies in the tongue. Words can build and can also tear down. You should never take too lightly the power of words. In view of the above, we should not use words in a slapdash fashion. Our speech must be seasoned with salt.

With so many things happening around the world, there is no shortage of talking points. People react differently to different political, social and economic evils that continue to beleaguer the entire globe. The words we utter in response to various crises expose, to a great extent, our level of maturity as well as our frame of mind.

There are people who are experts at complaining and whining about anything and everything. They even complain about situations for which they lack understanding. They blame the state for their poverty and all the wretchedness. They cast aspersions at government leaders and even solicit and lobby for a regime change. They live under the erroneous impression that it is the responsibility of the government to make them succeed in life.

The truth is that government does not owe you a living. The government is not there to purchase provisions for your family. It is your obligation to work hard and ensure that you put food on the table for you and your family; if you have one. Improve your sense of responsibility and stop lumping blame on the government of the day for supposedly being dysfunctional in life. If you do not change tack and realize that it is up to you to make wealth and not government, you keep on waiting for the government to serve your interests in perpetuity. You must understand that the government of heaven is ready to change your fortunes if you care to follow the ideology of kingdom economics.

There is an attitude you must display when responding to intricate and intractable circumstances. In life you must avoid mob psychology or group thinking. Decline to think the way everyone else is thinking. The way you think is very critical. It is out of our dominant thoughts that character is shaped. It is illusive to assume that you can achieve positive domino effects when your thinking is punctuated by pessimism.

Remember that you can never rise above your thoughts. You are what you think period. The Bible declares that as a man thinks so is he. Have pure, progressive thoughts and you will be amazed at the quantum leap you will make in life.

It is an open secret that nowadays, it is very complicated to tell the gap between Christians and the non-believers. This is because Christians are speaking the language of non-Christians. How does the world talk? They talk negatively and expect things to become positive just like that. They are arm chair critics.

When I was pursuing a Degree in Commerce (Finance and Accounts), the component on taxation seemed impossible for me to surmount. But because I developed a positive attitude towards the subject, I cleared it. I passed the subject despite having previously failed the first and second Continuous Assessment Tests. All I did was to pull myself together, study hard and maintain an affirmative frame of mind. I am now a proud holder of a degree in Commerce not because I am more intelligent than you. Through self-talk I would use my tongue to speak victory over the troublesome subject. Use words to prophesy success into your issues.

I am sure you are alive to the fact that many people today think being poor is the will of God for their lives. I wonder where they inherited this retrogressive doctrine from! They can be exonerated for not knowing that Jesus came here on earth to render null and void a number of spiritual phenomena.

It is important to restate the fact that Jesus paid the definitive price and sacrifice in order to reconcile man back to God and consequently restore man to his past position in God. He took away all the shame and everything that is not in keeping with the will of God the Father. Jesus, who knew no sin, became sin so that we may become the righteousness of God. On the cross, Jesus became poor so that we could become rich. For that reason, the Bible says, "let the poor say I am rich and the weak say I am strong" because of what the Lord has done!

Against this milieu, there is need for you to know who you are in God. Once you know and appropriate who you are in God, your perspectives on a number of issues that inform public discourse will change. It is a requisite for a believer to get knowledge and understanding of life and living. Though we are in this world, we are not of this world. Once you interface with this truth, you will learn to speak optimistically.

If you have nothing of substance to offer in a gathering, hold your peace and let well-informed people have the floor. The problem is not with God but with you. You have no control over your tongue. You speak whatever comes to your mind unguardedly. A child of God must circumspectly choose his words and speak with good judgment.

Reckless speaking has very far-reaching consequences. People have gotten themselves into trouble for not mincing their words. Others have made misfortunes befall their children because of parental name calling. Strive to be a father or mother that speaks good things into your children. A mature loving parent cannot sink so low as to call his own child a frog, dog or a fool. Always remember that words have creative as well as destructive power before you release them from your mouth. Speak life and not death.

It matters a lot how you respond to a crisis. It shows your level of maturity and faith in God. When God allows adverse circumstances in your life, He wants you to remain optimistic and cheerful if you know that He is able to work things for your good ultimately. When the wicked grumble and whine, do not add your voice to their expression of grief and curses against the powers that be. When the economy suffers a downward spiral, it is an occasion for you to plug into God's heavenly resources. You will prosper while others' fortunes are diminishing under the force of economic austerity.

It is in times of economic adversity that some people tend to conjure up brilliant business proposals. Predicaments do have a way of revealing positive traits in people. Be strong and do not leverage the adversary to wrap your dream in negativity. In all perilous times retain an affirmative attitude and thank God for every situation you maybe in. Keep in mind that all things work together for good to those who love the Lord and are called according to His purposes. In all trying times it is important to realize that God is still on the throne and that He is in control of any existing state of affairs.

CHAPTER EIGHTEEN
MAKE WISE DECISIONS

No one can dispute the fact that human beings are compelled to make decisions on a regular basis. Decision making is an integral and critical exercise to which we can all relate. We make decisions based on the nature of the problem and the use of available pertinent details. An informed decision is one that is information based and is therefore a coherent one.

We make decisions as we move on in our journey of life. We make decisions concerning food, clothing etc. Our actions in various areas of human endeavor are offshoots of our choices. What we become in life is the product and function of our daily decisions. Decisions or choices are the undercurrents of what transpires every day. There is nothing that happens by chance.

A decision is a decision whether bad or good. What determines the quality of a decision is its outcome or aftermath. Critical decisions require maturity and a measure of wisdom. That is why when you were young; all critical decisions were made for you. When you were young you were subject to parental guidance. However, when you attained the age of accountability, you were weaned and considered man or woman enough to make your own decisions. There is a sense in which you are left to your own devices. The danger though is that every decision taken has an impact on your future. Therefore, ensuring that you make wise decisions is a great aspect of your daily grind. Ensure that you make informed decision at every given opportunity.

Decisions can be self-serving or designed to address the greater picture. In view of the foregoing, when deciding, it is important to look at the envisaged benefits for you first as an individual as well as the community at large. A self-serving decision is one that benefits yourself alone at the expense of significant others. Let what you decide be of benefit to others also. That is why seeking advice is imperative in the decision-making process.

As a kingdom minded youth, what will distinguish you from your peers is the quality of decisions you make as an individual. You should aim at making influential and in-depth decisions. Be concerned with what goes on around you.

It is embarrassingly true that some people are poor today because of the poor decisions they made yesterday. If you take time to investigate the cause of some failed business ventures, your answers will gravitate towards bad decision making. For example, some companies fail to maximize profit primarily due to poor management policies and decisions. It is important not just to make decisions, but wise ones for that matter!

If large multi-national business concerns can go into liquidation owing to poor business decisions, what more an individual! Life is too short to accommodate errors. Be accountable for your decisions and actions. Today many young people are living with HIV simply because of poor choices in terms of moral propriety. They have gone against strong advice from their parents and peer educators by indulging in sex before marriage or worse still, having unprotected sex with a chain of sexual partners. The significance of making informed decisions cannot be overemphasized.

Accept who you are

"You are fearfully and wonderfully made."

(Psalm 139:14)

It is acknowledged that people come from different backgrounds with different mind sets, and different orientation. Some come from well to do families while others from vulnerable low-income households. This spawn's needless inferiority complexes in the poor and down trodden.

A classless society will remain a misleading notion. The world will always have rich people on one hand and the poor on the other. It is a known fact that some people are poor as a consequence of making poor choices in defining moments. By the same token some people have prospered in life because of having made good decisions. In order to have a balanced view, we cannot disregard the truth that some people are born rich by having inherited riches from their parents.

Some people have failed to excel in life because of having a poor self-image. The poor self-esteem may be originating from their perceived 'ugliness'. Persons with disabilities also tend to withdraw from critical areas of human activity, and hence miss out on business and other opportunities. Such people usually have a defective interpretation of life and may even be bitter with God.

Coming from a background of poverty does not necessarily mean that you will remain underprivileged for the rest of your life. You have a choice to either emancipate yourself from that environment of paucity or to accept your dismal circumstances as a normal phenomenon.

You must begin by declaring that poverty is not your portion. Set goals for your economic uplift and take deliberate steps towards achieving them. You may be underprivileged now but God looks at you in terms of the potential He has deposited in you. Have a dream and a vision that will change your story. You may start small but aim for higher heights. Do not despise your days of humble beginnings. Rome was not built in a day!!

People may classify and define you based on your current social status. But you can also define yourself according to what the Bible says you are. Your identity is in the word of God as opposed to public opinion. Delight yourself in the Lord and believe in your heart that God is about to do something great in your life.

Bear in mind that God made people differently. Apart from the common denominator, which is being made in the image of God, our particulars vary from one person to another. Your particulars and traits are not the same as those of your neighbor. Every person is unique and there are no carbon copies. The attributes you possess are not transferable. There will never be another you.

Use your gift and talent

What is it that one thing that you are very good at, your strong suit? Do not attempt to something God did not configure you for. Do not try to be a businessman when you clearly have neither grace nor sustainable interest in business. In church we have seen how people who have no musical ability insist on belonging to the church choir. It is necessary to ascertain what God created you to become rather than subject your life to trial and error.

There is a divine reason why God endowed you with the skills and competences that you have. Therefore, innovate around your gift and it will eventually cause you to prosper beyond your wildest dreams. It is important to know that the gift God has given you is predestined to be for the common good of your generation. If you elect to sit on it, you are in effect disadvantaging a lot of people who God intended to bless through you.

Your life in its entirety is designed to be a blessing to others. Your gift is a vital resource for living a fruitful and meaningful life. Once you discover and exploit your gift to great effect; you are headed for success and self-actualization.

Fight for what is right

"But David said to Saul, 'your servant has been keeping his father's sheep. When a lion or bear came and carried off a sheep from the flock, I went after it, struck it and rescued the sheep from its mouth. When it turned on me, I seized it by its hair, struck it and killed it. Your servant has killed both the lion

and the bear; this uncircumcised philistine will be one of them, because he has defied the armies of the living God. The Lord who delivered me from the paw of the lion and the paw of the bear will deliver me from the hands of this philistine."

(1 Samuel 17:34-37)

No matter your background and your current social economic status, you were created to fulfill God's purposes. Your birth was neither a mistake nor an accident. God knew you even before you were formed in your mother's womb. And so, the significance of determining your gifts and talents cannot be overemphasized. There is always one person that has, through their gifting, a lasting solution to an existing problem in the community. There are many issues in life that require specific solutions. All the challenges and problems we face in the community are solved by someone simply exercising and applying his God given gift. You are part of society hence you owe your society a service which only you, through your gift can offer.

There are issues which are meant to be solved by a group or by an individual. Exhibition of lethargy and apathy in solving community or individual's problems is a retrogressive phenomenon. Always bear in mind that God intended for you to be a solution giver according to your gifting.

1 Samuel 17:35-37 shows us how David refused to keep quiet about a national crisis for which he knew he had capacity to deal with. All and sundry in the entire nation were afraid to take up the challenge; including the king. If you know you have a solution to a disturbing problem, do not fold your arms and expect others to rise to the occasion.

If you are the right person to handle a particular problem, God will typically put a burden upon your heart and you better not close your eyes to the promptings of God. There is potential for greatness in your genes and chromosomes! Exhaust all the possibilities entrenched in; that God given potential while you still have your being. If you are a singer, do not die with a song in your mouth!

Peer pressure

"Do not be deceived; evil communication corrupts good manners."

(1 Corinthians 15:33)

Peer pressure is a phenomenon that has the potential to wreak havoc particularly among youths. This is so because young people are so susceptible and naïve and their perception of life is influenced by their infantile behavior. Peer pressure can either be positive or negative. The kind of peer pressure applied in a particular context is understandably identified by the end result. Negative peer pressure occurs when a group or an individual get influenced in a pessimistic way. A young person can, for example start smoking cigarettes simply because all his classmates are into that habit. He somehow is led to believe that smoking is a sign of being 'smart'. He for that reason aspires to identify with the rest of the class. Destinies are miscarried as a product of negative peer pressure.

In Contrast, positive peer pressure can ultimately position a person in the trajectory of his destiny. The same manner that a friend can mislead you, a friend can equally offer constructive pressure. So be careful about the company you keep. Bad company spoils good morals!

You may not feel the devastating effects of negative peer pressure in the immediate wake of its application. The truth is, its consequences always come full circle. It is common knowledge that the friends that we hang out with on a daily basis do have some direct and indirect influence on our lives. Your friends are mirror images of who you are!

In life we have no choice about which family to be born into. But in creating friendships, the choice is ours. Let your circle of friends be the catalyst to the fulfillment of your dream and the launch pad to your greatness.

Proverb

"Show me your friend and I will tell you who you are."

It is unattainable to remain upright and dignified when you have sited your life in a circle of corrupt friends. You cannot be in a bad and corrupt company and remain honest. Unquestionably, some people have experienced negative behavioral change upon befriending people with questionable conduct. The reverse benefit they get from such friends is simply bad influence. If you neglect the advice about choosing friends wisely, your so called friends will be used by the devil to pull you down and drag your name through the muck.

Not every person you meet is first-rate material for companionship. Some people are strategically planted by the devil along your path of destiny to play the role of detractors. Choose your friends in discerning manner and you will not play into the hands of villains. Abstain from hanging out with peers that have a contrary spirit. There is a high chance that they are undercover agents of the devil. Flee from such without thinking twice.

In addition, you have to understand that your parents love you and that they invested a lot into your life even at the expense of their own comfort. So, as you move on with your life, ensure that you do not break the hearts of your parents. After your parents have done everything in their power to raise you into a decent and responsible child, do not invalidate their many years of parenting by yielding to negative peer pressure. Many Parents have suffered anguish after seeing their son or daughter experience a negative behavioral swing all because of keeping bad company. They cannot stomach or figure out the abrupt twist of fate in their child's life.

A good child aims to please and impress his/her parents because parents always have high expectations from their offspring. If you are a youth and you are exhibiting uncharacteristic behavior, consider changing for the better. There is still room for you to make amends. Your potential to become great and leaving positive footprints in the sands of history can be totally wasted because you choose to throw caution to the wind by living an out of control life.

Take a deep breath and reflect on the class and caliber of the people you call friends. Start by listing their names and conduct an exhaustive integrity test on each one of them. Those that do not make the grade must be unfriended without delay, to use a Face book expression!

Under normal circumstances, a friend is supposed to add value to your life. Those that are bent of diminishing your level of integrity and human decency must have their names struck off the register of associates.

Some people stoop to peer pressure in order to avoid losing friends. On the road to greatness you have no alternative but to disassociate yourself from certain friends. You are better off walking alone than being encircled by immoral friends. Take a bold stand for your convictions. Your dream to succeed should embolden you to get rid of twisted friends. If you decide to dismiss dreadful friends, you can be sure that God will connect you to the right ones. Trust God even where selection of friendship is concerned.

Aim high

"Brothers, I do not consider myself yet to have taken hold of it. But one thing I do; forgetting what is behind and straining towards what is ahead."

(Philippians 3:13)

As a rule, individuals with a vision always set their sights very high. They set their sights high enough such that their eyes overlook all the dire circumstances that comprise the status quo. They know that the stakes are very high and therefore they become as bold as a lion, knowing the blessings that await them. God has already set your trajectory and itinerary for your life. Therefore, if there is a crisis on the way, it is not with God but most likely with you!

Learn to ask God to reveal His will over your life. God is ready when you are ready. In as much as God has got good plans for your life, devotedly playing your part is a fundamental dynamic. You play your part by living according to what is demanded of you by your maker.

Oftentimes, people pray that God could change the circumstances that encase their lives. The trouble is that many of such people are not willing to pay the price. For anything good to take place in one's life, there is always a price to pay and a process to undergo. For example, if you want to pass an exam, you will have to make sure that you study hard.

Fair enough, even with the things of God, there are sacrifices to be made. The road to success puts a lot of demands on us, making the likelihood of giving up incredibly high. I am sure you have heard stories of people aspiring to get rich opting to solicit help from fortune-tellers! All they are told is to make a sacrifice and that sacrifice is what supposedly determines the amount of money they will receive once the ritual is over.

But with God, the sacrifice He will require from you is obedience to His statutes as well as staying the course even in times of dispiriting conditions. He knows that by His sufficient grace you can afford to make that sacrifice.

In *john 8:1-11*, Jesus told a woman who was caught committing adultery that her sins had been forgiven and that she should go and put an end to her sinful life. In your life's journey, fix your eyes on Jesus and your mind on the cross. Do not look to the right or to the left. Look straight ahead and you shall see the salvation of the Lord.

CHAPTER NINETEEN
YOU CAN BOUNCE BACK

"Then he found the jawbone of a donkey that had recently died. He bent down and picked it up and killed a thousand men with it."

(Judges15:15)

Our featured scripture shows us that Samson was a man whom God had chosen and raised to deliver Israel from the Philistines. He carried a divine responsibility which was bestowed on him at birth. God had ordained him to be the deliverer of Israel from her adversaries. Samson was anointed with the spirit of extraordinary valor that empowered and motivated him to do unbelievable exploits for God. Samson did things which conventional strength could not possibly accomplish.

An analytical look at Samson's notable accomplishments provides irrefutable evidence that God was truly with him in all his undertakings. God's helping hand in Samson's life can be replicated in your life as well. Samson was equal to the task in terms of defending the people of Israel. This was his life assignment given him by God. Nothing can be closer to the truth than to state that you also have a specific assignment to carry out in order to fulfill Kingdom purposes. For every assignment God supplies the pertinent skill set to necessitate and guarantee its successful completion.

It is safe to insist that we are all born to carry out a cross section of Kingdom purposes. Against this background, the unearthing of your assignment and the ability to perform it are two very important talking points in your life. What you were born to do is what matters at the end of the day. You could be an accountant, pastor, social worker, engineer or student, but the paramount thing is to know your particular area of operation that fits into your dream!

"Then she shouted! "Samson the philistines are coming!" he woke up and thought, he "I will get loose and get free as always." He did not know that the Lord had left him. The philistines captured him and put his eyes out. They took him to Gaza, chained him with bronze chains and put him to work grinding at the mill in prison."

(Judges16:20-21)

Regardless of Samson being anointed and accredited with a divine mandate, he made a very detrimental gaffe which put his life in serious jeopardy. He shared classified information with a wrong person concerning the secret behind his extraordinary power. His power was a huge source of apprehension for a long time in the Philistine corridors of power. In a moment of pure madness while in the warm embrace of Delilah's arms, Samson divulged the secret of his rare strength to her. It can be conjectured Samson did not at the moment realize the severity of the consequences of his action. As far as he was concerned, he was merely attesting his inimitable love and trust for his mistress.

But we later read about the calamitous consequences of his historic blunder. Delilah eventually betrayed him by covertly conveying that vital detail to the Philistines. The misery that ensued in Samson's life subsequently is too horrific to contemplate. He went through a sequence of distressing and agonizing events.

 The lesson we gather from Samson's ordeal is that you should desist from sharing information especially concerning your private particulars to people who do not have your best interests at heart. Mind the people you share information with; more especially where dreams are concerned. Guard your God given vision jealously because a lot of people that you meet along the way may be emissaries of Satan sent to overturn your destiny.

Not all your colleagues are genuine friends. Hence be very careful with some people. There is always a Judas among your circle of friends. Some people may be laughing with you, but that does not mean they are happy with the shrewdness you possess and what you are capable of doing. People who do not mean well for your life will always be there. Use your gift of discernment to identify such deceivers in your life!

One of the disastrous ramifications in Samson's betrayal by his ostensible concubine was that his eyes were ruthlessly gouged out by his adversaries. Needless to mention, he became utterly blind. The loss of sight must have elated his nemeses a great deal. Stripped of his hair and eyesight, he no longer posed any credible menace to them. Because of his failure to maintain secrecy with regard to his source of strength, Samson lost his comparative advantage over his foes. He became sightless and powerless simultaneously. He went through unimaginable emotional and physical pain.

You could be in a similar situation; feeling distraught and despondent as you sit at the dining table of consequences. You feel all hope is gone and there is nothing to live for! You have a number of regrets and counting your losses because of what you did. Stop lamenting over spilt milk and pull yourself together again. The past has passed and it is time to regroup and chart the way forward. A righteous man can fall seven times and seven times he will rise again.

Re-focus and revisit your dream again! You have to know that God is able to deliver you from all disasters. He is a God of the second chance. The devil wants you to remain whining and wallowing in the muck of regrets. God has not given up on you!

"Then Samson prayed, "sovereign Lord, please remember me; give me my strength just once more, so that with this one blow I can get even with the philistines for putting out my two eyes. So, Samson took hold of the two middle pillars holding up the building. Putting one hand on each pillar, he pushed against them. And shouted, "Let me die with the philistines" he pushed with all his might and the building fell down on the five kings and everyone else. Samson killed more people at his death than he had killed during his life."

(Judges 16:28-30)

The underlying factor here is to perceive what prayer can do. After Samson had been stripped bare of his singular attributes, his enemies were under the impression that they had seen the last of the son of Manoah. The great Samson whom the Lord had raised to deliver Israel from the hands of her enemies was now blind. He was at that juncture incapable to fight the philistines because he now reduced to a prisoner of war.

There is always a way forward in situations where there seems to be no hope. I believe prayer is what is necessary for the Lord God Almighty to intervene and show Himself strong on your behalf. Call upon the name of the Lord and He will surely come to your rescue. Prayer changes situations!

Despite living under the specter and consequences of his costly oversight, Samson didn't bury his head in the sand, but prayed to the Lord to strengthen him once more. This is a definitive example of how a strong-minded   person should respond to any catastrophe in life.

Hope in God should be maintained at all costs. It is important to never give up in life. Your losses can be turned into gains provided you trust the Lord unreservedly. In fact, you can spring back and scale to even higher heights than you did before. The story of Job is a stark reminder that God can restore your fortunes. Confront every mistake and challenge it with fervent prayer and God's word. It is only the word of God that can change things in your life. Speak the prophetic word of God for a better tomorrow.

God empowered Samson to kill more people at the time of his death than he did in his whole lifetime. Don't limit God for He is able to change any condition for the better. He makes a way where there seems to be no way.

"Joseph gave orders to fill his brother's packs with corn, to each man's money back in his sack and to give them food for the journey. This was done. The brothers loaded their donkeys with the corn they had bought and then left."

(Genesis42; 25-26)

As a result of your past actions, people might have given up on you and cast aspersions on you. Let me say it for the umpteenth time; don't give up on your dreams. Be strong and courageous. Do you know that some people's fortunes are connected to your life? It simply means that when you give up on your dream you are affecting many other people's lives.

It is important for you to know that there a lot of people out there looking up to you. Consider your country, friends and family. Peradventure you may be the one to deliver your family from cyclical generational poverty. When you keep this picture in mind; you will not default of your dream or assignment because the stakes are very high. It has been submitted that obstacles are what you see when you take your eyes off your goal.

"The Lord reached down from above and took hold of me; he pulled me out of the deep waters. He rescued me from my powerful enemies and from all those who hate me."

(Psalm 18:16-17)

The God who placed that vision or dream in you will be faithful to consummate it. Above and beyond; your dream once fulfilled will be an enhancement to Kingdom purposes. Hence trust in God for all the strength, direction and resources prerequisite for the actualization of your dream. He is more than able to do exceedingly abundantly above which you can ask and imagine.

In as much as you want your dream to come true, God wants you to maintain godliness with contentment as you patiently but readily look forward to your breakthrough. He also wants you happy about today and not wishing for so called old days. Just keep confessing that where you are today is not where you will be tomorrow. God is renowned for taking His children from one degree of glory to another!

"Who shall separate us from the love of the Christ? Shall tribulation, or distress, or persecution, or famine, or nakedness or peril, or sword? Nay, in all these things we are more than conquerors through him that loved us."

(Romans 8:35-37)

The God we serve knows the end from the beginning. The Lord already knows the end result of whatever adversity you are grappling with in your life. One thing you can take away from **Romans 8:35-37** is that nothing should make you give up on anything. Decline to allow any consequence to douse the joy of the Lord which is your strength in any given situation.

Learn to use God's word to your advantage. God has placed in you a gift, talent, ideas that cannot be photocopied. The Bible says the gift of a man will make room for him and usher him in the presence of great men. Apply your skills to the best of your ability knowing full well that once you are blessed you will be a blessing to other people. Know that you are inhibiting other people's destinies by failing to take full advantage of your potential.

That was then

"Brothers, I do not consider myself yet to have taken hold of it. But one thing I do; forgetting what is behind and straining towards what is ahead."

(Philippians 3:13)

"And God is able to make all grace abound to you, that always having all sufficiency in everything; you may have abundance for every good deed."

(2 Corinthians 9:8)

Regardless of your past failures and inconsistencies, every new day is an opportunity for you to make amends. God's mercies are new every morning. Overlook the bygones and focus on your future. Our past failures form the basis of our wise choices today. Despite your litany of failures in the past the truth still remains, and that is, God has a ladder to your destiny already lined up!

Instead of indulging in self-pity and self-condemnation, surrender all your burdens to God and He will gladly supply a new meaning to your life. Meditating on your past failures, misfortunes and pain can suppress the joy of expecting good things in future. In a nutshell, forget the past and be inspired by the prospect of success. Make more use of the windscreen than the rear-view mirror! Do not live in the past. Your best days are still yet to come.

God can give you a new beginning and a fresh perspective of life. He is not limited by anything. He quickens the dead and calls those things which are not as though they were. *Romans 4:17*

"So, confess your sins to one another and pray for one another so that you may be healed. The prayer of a righteous person has great effectiveness."

(James5:16)

Let me go over the significance of disregarding the past if you are looking to move forward. Desist from feeding your mind with painful accounts from your past. Relish the possibility of making it big in life. By developing such a mental attitude, you will be transformed from the detrimental impact of the past.

Furthermore, bear in mind that the devil is a liar. His mission is to kill, steal and destroy. He is hell bent on reminding you about what transpired in the past; your past misfortunes; stuff that you would rather forget! The bottom line is that he does not mean well for your life. The devil has never sent a goodwill message to any soul. He doesn't want you happy about life. He wants you to give up on that which will bless many for generations to come. *(John 10:10)*

You have to accept that the past has passed and never to revisit again. Your major concern now is to taper your focus on the future. We are all alive to the fact that it is rather easier said than done to forget the past. But forgetting is the best policy going forward.

How can I forget my past one may ask? Start by forgiving yourself and all those who may have wronged you. When you forgive, you effectively emancipate yourself from the prison of acrimony. When you keep grudges, it is you that suffer and not the individual who hurt your feelings. Holding on to past adversities robs you the joys of today and the imminent thrills of the future.

Know who can be of help and have a will to live

"And a certain woman, who had an issue of blood for twelve years, and had suffered many things of many physicians, and had spent all that she had, and was nothing bettered, but rather grew worse. When she had heard of Jesus, came in the press behind, and touched his garment. For she said, if I may touch but his clothes, I shall be whole. And straightway the fountain of her blood dried up; and she felt in her body that she was healed of that plague."

(Mark 5:25-29)

As earlier alluded to, life can be such a heavy stack of traumatic episodes.

When under the pressure of undesirable circumstances, you may be prompted to ask, why me? Why now? And what sin did I commit? This is always a heartbreaking position to be in. The story of the woman who suffered from an issue of blood sums up what I am trying to say here. She tried her best to find a remedy for her embarrassing condition but to no avail. Nothing good could come out of her efforts even after spending a lot on medical expenses. The more she tried the more her condition deteriorated. If this particular story had no joyful conclusion, it would have ranked among the gloomiest accounts in the Bible!

You have to put yourself in her shoes for you to appreciate the torment and affliction she underwent. Just see in your mind's eye how she spent all her investments on medical bills with no improvement. She tried everything in her power to salvage her fitness with nothing to show for her concerted efforts. Her life was at a knife edge. Have you ever been in situations where everything that can go wrong has gone wrong?

The crux of the matter is that this woman never lost hope even for a fleeting moment. That clarifies why she kept moving from doctor to doctor. She was determined against all odds to have her health restored. It was that resilience and conviction that eventually connected her to Jesus. The culmination of her conviction was her game-changing encounter with Jesus. Her story changed and the rest is history. Where there is a will there is a way.

One notable trait about this woman is her perseverance, tenacity and doggedness! She was steadfast in her resolve to be whole again and enjoy life like any other person in her community. The other thing worth mentioning is that she was sick and tired of that debilitating condition. She did not keep quiet about it or believe the situation a normal thing. She could no longer put up with the stigma and humiliation from people's comments. She was the typical subject of community gossip.

Until you realize you need help, help may never come your way. For that reason, being cognizant of people who can render help to you is the first step to discovering the solution. Always recognize and accept your lack of capacity in order to seek the indulgence of those that have the knowledge and skill relevant to your predicament. Appreciating and recognizing other people's competences does not necessarily mean they are better human beings than you. A smart person is one who is able to identify a talent in another person's life and connect with such people. Swallow your narcissism and acknowledge your boundaries. You cannot be a jack of all trades.

It is tremendously imperative to know the attributes of Jesus. All power belongs to Him and with Him there is nothing impossible. What is impossible with man is possible with Him. When you have a personal encounter with Him your life can never be the same again.

You should come to a point of realization that something has to change in your life. Your challenge could be financial, medical, academic, and spiritual etc. Provided your problem has a name, it shall certainly stoop to the name that is above all names; Jesus. Trust God with all your heart and He will supply all your needs according to His riches in glory. He is more than able to deliver you from any kind of problem.

Consequently, ask for help from those who can help. Similarly, render help to those who need help. This is not just a mere advice; it is a biblical a norm. "He that waters others shall himself be watered" (**Proverb 11:25**).

What is it that is not giving you peace? Bring it to God and see how great and mighty He is.

"And when heard that it was Jesus of Nazareth, he began to cry out, and say, Jesus, thou son David, have mercy on mw. And many charged him to that he should hold his peace; but he cried the more a great deal, thou son of David, have mercy on me. And Jesus stood still, and commended him to be called there. And they called the blind man, saying unto him, be of good comfort, rise; he calleth thee. And he, casting away his garment, rose and came to Jesus. And Jesus answered and said unto him, what wilt thou that I should do unto thee? The blind man said unto him, lord, that I may receive my sight. And Jesus said unto to him, go thy way; thy faith hath made thee whole. And immediately he received his sight, and followed Jesus in the way."

(Mark 10:47-52)

In order to live a fulfilled life, it is pivotal to identify people whose contribution can thrust you towards your destiny. The minute you realize that no man is an island and thus acknowledge the need for interaction with other people, you will literally broaden your horizons and open yourself to an avalanche of opportunities.

The story read in **Mark 10:47-52** provides a practical insight on how one can be helped. It moreover confirms that those who seek help will surely find it. If you know people that can help advance your agenda well and good. You are off to a good start. To put a caveat to this however, make sure they are the right people in terms of their integrity and authenticity. If you harbor reservations about them, think twice before a blunder is made. Many people have fallen victim to people they confided in with the hope of being helped. So exercise extreme discretion as you look for destiny helpers.

In **Psalms 23:1-6**, King David says, "the Lord is his shepherd; I shall not want." David is simply granting that he has one shepherd who always meets his daily needs. The Psalmist declares that he can never lack anything as long as the Lord remains his shepherd. Having a problem and knowing how it should be solved are two different things. Therefore, one must have the capacity to identify the problem first before seeking help.

The following points may be of help in problem solving;

1. **Problem recognition**
   Before anything else, you need to recognize the problem. For you cannot fight what you don't know.
2. **Identifying the problem**
   After recognizing a problem, you need to identify it in specific terms. Once the problem has been recognized and identified, the next step is to identify who can help you.
3. **Evaluation of helpers**

Once you have come to know the problem, you should be able to know who can help you. It has to be someone you can trust, is mature and you know them very well.

4. *Help found*

After all the tabulated steps have been followed, you should be able to find help. So, take heart and know that all things work together for good to those who love the Lord and are called according to His purposes. Continue believing that your status quo is not permanent. Your story shall change.

CHAPTER TWENTY

ACCEPT WHERE YOU COME FROM

Accepting where you are coming from in relation to who you are today is a needful thing to do. Having been born in a poor family is an opportunity for you to break your family's generational cycle of poverty. You can purpose in your heart to be the first successful businessman in your family. Be proud of mentioning that you are coming from a poor background so that when you break the jinx the whole world will hear about you.

During my high school days, there was a boy who claimed to have been coming from a rich family. He told us he was living in some affluent residential area in Lusaka. He could tell us stories regarding the purported residential area located in the heart of Lusaka.

 Going by his stories, everyone took for granted that indeed he was from a well to do family. We admired him a great deal and we all knew it was cool to live in those quiet clean residential areas.

Little did we know that the chap's stories were just a fabrication. This is what happened. One day I visited someone who was my junior in school. What I saw shocked me to the core. This guy truly lived in some cool residential area in the heart of Lusaka with some neighbors being high ranking government officials.

I was so impressed and my heart was filled with joy. When we entered the gate, I was so eager to enter the big house but the opposite happened. This guy took me in the backyard to a small two-roomed quarter. I wondered what was happening but I could not ask what was going on. My host was actually leading me to the house where the other guy used to live.

To cut the story short, I met his loving and caring mum who wanted nothing but the best for her son and guess what? I never told anyone in school when we opened. This guy thought I was going to expose him but he never heard me tell anyone about 'his rich family in some expensive place' in Lusaka.

Coming from a poor background is not your fault. You didn't choose to be born in a poor family. You didn't choose your parents but God did. There is nothing wrong to be born in a poor family but there is something wrong in remaining poor even after coming to know the truth; and how to come out of poverty.

Accept that you are from an underprivileged family but declare that by the grace of God I will change the story of my family. Acknowledge your parents' sacrificial efforts of giving you good education.

One of the most foolish things one can ever do is to be ashamed of his parents simply because they are poor. Stories have been told about people who have denied their shabby looking parents in public. Some have the temerity to take other people to represent them on momentous occasions when it should be their parents' pleasure and right to do so. Your parents must be respected and praised for raising and sending you to school through sweat and toil. They deserve to be honored and celebrated!

How can a sane person be ashamed of his/her parents, who made untold sacrifices to make them what they are today? Today you cannot even visit your parents because they still live in a shanty compound which is too low for your 'level'. In a nutshell, honor your father and mother so that you may be blessed with long life.

Your parents went out of their way to ensure your welfare. Sometimes they went hungry so that the little food that was on hand could be set aside for you. Let no man born of a woman cause you to forget how your parents starved for your sake. For those who are married do not let your wife separate you from your parents. Don't forget your parents and don't make them cry because of you have neglected them. In conclusion, the problem is neither where you are coming from nor your shabby poor parents. The problem is with you for failing to accept that you once lived in squalor and today you have the cheek to look down on people who are still living there.

CHAPTER TWENTY ONE

PERMIT YOURSELF TO BE HAPPY

Once in a while take time to mull over the kind of life you are leading. Analyze it in light of God's word and see if its current quality is what is designated in the word. Is it pleasing and acceptable before God Almighty? How is it benefiting others in the body of Christ? Are you truly contented with the kind of life that you are leading now or not?

All things are permissible but not all are expedient. There are things which really have affirmative benefits in one's life and serve as insurance for a brighter future. It is important to live a purpose-driven life while bearing in mind that one day we shall all give an account about what we invested our lives into.

Many people today, particularly the youth, are not living right both in the eyes of God and their parents. Many young people are caught up in riotous living. They do not care how they live their lives and they seem to be oblivious to the impending ramifications of the behavior.

The older generation is to a degree to blame for the irresponsible behavior of youths. Our parents, uncles and aunts do not come out in the open to rebuke young people. If they do, they do it guardedly and with reservations. Besides, some old people exhibit the same behavior as that exemplified by young people. Some old men do openly have illicit love affairs with girls of the same age as their own daughters. By the same token, there are old women who flirt with boys of the same age as their biological sons. This sort of conduct is absolutely outrageous and disgusting.

Swayed by the pleasures of this world, some people have traded their spiritual birth right just like Esau did in the Bible. By indulging in worldly pleasures, they have compromised their relationship with God. They have traded the joy of the Lord for the misleading distractions of this world.

True contentment and fulfillment do not derive from the amusements of this world. The devil has from time immemorial conned people into thinking that there is nothing wrong with 'having a good time.'

God wants you to live a life of peace and happiness on His terms. Don't allow yourself to be unhappy because of what happened in the past. Do not allow your past experiences to rob you of your present joy. Jesus came that you may have life and have it in abundance. Happiness lies in knowing your savior; knowing that your sins are forgiven!

On no account should you trade your happiness for anything. Be the man of virtue, honesty and totally devoted to God. Be wary that the pleasures of this world are intended to sidetrack people from the proper contentment that can only be found in God.

CHAPTER TWENTY TWO
THE POWER OF DESTINY

Throughout this book the theme has been about God having a plan and purpose for you here on earth. Let this reality lodge and inhabit in your spirit. The fact that God has a destiny for you is a foregone conclusion. The race to your destiny starts the day you yield your life to Jesus Christ and begin to walk in newness of life. Whatsoever you were formed for is calculated to stimulate glory to God. The Bible says we were created for his pleasure.

"And Samuel to Jesse, are these all the children? And he said, there remaining yet youngest, and behold, he is tending the sheep! Then Samuel said to Jesse, send and bring him; for we will not sit down until he comes here. So he sent and brought him in. Now he was ruddy, with beautiful eyes and a handsome appearance. And the Lord said "arise, anoint him for this is he"

(1 Samuel 16:11-12)

"Then Samuel said to David, you are not able to go against this philistine to fight with him; for you are but a youth while he has been a warier from his youth."

(1 Samuel 17:33)

As believers we are people of destiny. Destiny connotes the events that will unavoidably occur to a particular person in future. It is the hidden power that controls future events. In other words, destiny is a predetermined future. That's why you cannot successfully run away from your destiny. Before you were conceived in your mother's womb, God had already made graphic representation of your life. The agenda is already set for you and you need to do is to resonate with it through spiritual sensitivity. Your work is already cut out. As soon as you discover the itinerary to your destiny, you will hit the ground running.

The story of David makes very interesting reading. David was an ordinary simple boy, doing the menial work of tending his father's sheep. It never crossed anyone's mind that David was destined for prominence. He started running the affairs of his father's business at a very tender age. With perception after the fact, we see that all the work he did diligently in his father's house was God's policy of grooming him for imminent kingship. Through the unattractive task of shepherding, David started developing a sense of responsibility and commitment. In the Kingdom of God great things come from small things (**Mark 4:31-32**). And in **Zachariah 4:10** the Lord loves small beginnings.

At the time Samuel was looking to anoint the next king of Israel from the house of Jesse, David was not even in the picture because everyone considered him as an insignificant person. There was virtually no basis on which anyone could think of him as royal material. He had a very undesirable profile and CV.

Because destiny has a way of locating people, his disentitlement (in the eyes of men) could not impede David from eventually being anointed by Samuel. Samuel insisted that David should be recalled from the bush where, as usual, tending his father's sheep. The moment David arrived home and appeared before Saul, there was an authentication that he was indeed the one to be anointed.

 No matter where you may be, be it in a rural area like Shangombo or in a sprawling city like New York, destiny will still find you. God is so mindful of you that He never left anything to chance. He made a bespoke package for your life. He knows how you will be from the end to the beginning. Just ensure that you position yourself strategically.

You should also understand that all these indicators start manifesting when you are young. Mostly, when you are young, that's when dreams and visions of your future and destiny are ministered in your heart as your relationship with God grows. There is nothing wrong in dreaming big and no one will ever question you for dreaming big. God gives dreams to young people for early preparation. Be excited that you are still youthful with so much vigor to accomplish amazing success.

"Let no one look down on your youthfulness, but rather in speech, conduct love, faith and purity. Show yourself an example of those who believe."

(1Timothy 4:12)

Formative years are a critical stage in a person's life. Adolescence is a period in which many young people would want to experiment with life. Many out of curiosity begin to sample alcohol, drugs, sex and drugs. Many compromise their potential just at this point in their development as human beings. With proper parental guidance many pass though this stage unscathed by peer pressure. These are the ones who later in life become high-flying citizens.

The youth stage sees a number of girl children dropping out of school due to early pregnancies. This trend is a vexing problem in our country. Girl children lose opportunities to get educated and live a decent life.

As read in *1Timothy 4:12,* youth stage should not be a justification or passport for one to experiment with sex, beer drinking or any other social vices. Instead it should be a phase in which one has to live an exemplary life. It is the stage when careers are discovered and character development begins.

Don't allow yourself to be deceived by a few minutes of pleasure that have the potential to blow your future away. Never allow anything to endanger your preordained future.

Say no to any social activity that may rein in your future and relegate you to a life of perpetual misery. Remember your creator when you are still a youth, in your heydays! Refuse to compromise your moral footing. You must not be ignorant of the devil's devices. He only comes to steal, kill and destroy.

CHAPTER TWENTY THREE

DON'T SIDELINE YOURSELF

The default theme of our discourse has been that you are special and unique. You are the apple of God's eye and you occupy a special place in His loving heart. The devil knows about your strong relationship with God and that is why he is always conducting attacks on you relentlessly. His intention is that you should shift your focus from God to your adversities.

The devil is always on a crusade designed to make God's children shift their attention to things that diminish their fellowship with God. The devil comes to steal, kill and destroy. The devil's ministry and agenda is to bring you down completely so that you begin to grow resentment against God. But Jesus has other plans. He will not allow the enemy to triumph over us. He came so that we might have life and have it in abundance.

Every person is a trendsetter and leader in his/her own area of strength. A doctor becomes a leader when there is something relating to health and healthy living. This is because of his or her specialization in the health sector. When it comes to finance and accounts, an accountant takes charge.

Every field of study gives one the mandate to lead at a particular time depending on what skill is needed at the material time. This truth makes everyone an important person. Every field of study is important and you are important. There is no field of study that is more significant than the others. Accountants need human resource personnel and human resource need experts in information technology. The point here is; you are also important because you are a leader in your own field of knowledge.

When there is need for prayer, a clergyman takes charge. This as I mentioned earlier makes everyone important and a leader according to the prevailing situation. Leadership to some extent is situational. A situation is what requires specific application of certain skill or knowledge making leadership situational.

There should be nothing to make you feel inferior. God sees in you a potential commissioner for His Kingdom duties. Don't allow any person to write you off because God has already ordained you for a specific assignment.

Nobody has the final say over your life apart from God. He alone has got the blueprint for your life. He already has a bill of quantities for the equipment you require on your life's journey.

Stop sidelining yourself and put your name on top. You may not have what it takes today but remember, your tomorrow will be better than your today. Today you may not have the required educational qualifications but you have the chance and opportunity to change your status. People might have written you off but don't pay attention to such. God calls the unqualified and qualifies the called.

God has the tendency of choosing the foolish things of this world in order to confound the wise. Nobody has the power to make you what you ought to be apart from God. Be available for God's business and your story will be a different one with time. Remember, God is not a respecter of persons. God can use any body He feels is ready and capable enough to deliver positive results.

You are one in a million and your story can change for the better. The best thing you can do is to allow God to do what He wants with your life and I can assure you without any doubt in my heart that your story will change. Don't underestimate the power of God over your life because God has the power to give life to dead situations.

CHAPTER TWENTY FOUR

FINISH WHAT YOU STARTED

Being the first to start any venture is not a guarantee that you will automatically be the first to finish as well. Before you embark on a project, ensure to count the cost and apply the principles of strategic management. Many people today seem not to know how to carry out the business dream in sustainable manner.

Some companies too may fail to achieve certain goals and objectives due to poor or defective policies. Everyday somebody somewhere is launching their dream company but few ventures survive the test of time. Personal relationships on the other hand have also been started and ended quickly and unceremoniously. This chapter is dedicated to presenting viable advice on how to start something that will come to its logical conclusion.

The first step to success is to identify what you want to achieve. Then go further to determine whether you have capacity to achieve your set goals. You also need to ascertain whether you can achieve your set goals single handedly or you would require have synergy with other parties.

Furthermore, sincerely establish the motive for you wanting to accomplish that particular goal. Ask yourself if you are inspired by self-serving desires, and if it is really necessary to achieve what you want to achieve. Determine if the desired goal is a constituent of your ministry and how it will be of benefit to others. Your sincere and up-front response to this inquisitiveness will be of tremendous help to you.

As mentioned already, every day people consistently coming up with different visions and goals to achieve. Some may even be the first to start and end up being last. This is because being the first to start something is not a guarantee that you will equally finish first. God desires people who are strategic in their way of doing things. Being smart is what will leverage you to finish first and strong.

People get so unreasonably thrilled when starting something new. They rejoice and think they have arrived without realizing that starting is one thing and finishing is another. Starting ahead of others has no bearing on the finishing point. However, finishing first and accomplishing great things has everything to do with the starting point.

What do I mean, you may ask? If starting first is what determines finishing first, how is that those who were ahead of you are now lagging behind? This should give you new perspectives about life. Don't be in a hurry to go about things. Hold your horses and ensure that everything that is required in finishing is in place. Vigilance is pivotal. Imagine a peasant farmer going to the field without a hoe. Footballers in the starting lineup always walk onto the football pitch dressed in full attire while those on the bench are never in fully outfitted.

Life requires you to have a good and strong foundation; rooted in the word of God. People who finish and accomplish their goals are always on point. Their goal and mission are always clear enough even for a grade seven pupil to understand. Having big and 'complicated' goals does not guarantee you the results. On the other hand, setting simple and clear goals is one of the steps to achievement.

Quitters never win and as a matter of fact, they are never recognized by society. Some people start well but get dispirited and frustrated along the way. In other words, they start well but finish badly, if at all we can call that 'finishing'. This is one of the intrigues of life. How do you join a marathon race and run out of steam in its very early stages? You need to count the cost of whatever business enterprise you desire to undertake and steer clear of the 'foolish virgin' syndrome. Do not consider quitting when you have the potential of reaching the finishing line. The completion of a mission is in the starting! On the social scene, why let go of that beautiful young lady or handsome man just because of one misunderstanding? How many relationships are you going to indulge in before you settle the issue of marriage?

To bottom line the matter, plan well before you start something in life. Planning takes care of all unforeseen circumstances and contingencies.

"This is what the LORD says- your Redeemer, the Holy One of Israel: "I am the LORD your God, who teaches you what is best for you, who directs you in the way you should go.

(Isaiah 48:17)

When he had finished speaking, he said to Simon, 'put out into deep water, and let down the nets for a catch. Simon answered, 'master, we have worked all night have not caught anything. But because you say so, I will let down the nets. When they had done so, they caught such a large number of fish that their nets began to break."

(Luke 5:4-6)

The remarkable story of Simon is an excellent paradigm of what I am striving to put across. On an ordinary night, Simon in the company of his fellow fishermen, ventured into the sea full of his typical confidence of knocking off with a good catch of fish. Unfortunately, the night turned out to be his worst nightmare. After applying all his experience and fishing dexterity, he sailed back to the shore empty handed. There was no anticipated catch. This just was not his night.

While Peter was clearing out his nets, a lot of thoughts were racing through his mind. He did not know what had hit him in spite of his optimism and all the logistics that go with his trade. As fate would have it, Jesus Christ appeared on the scene. True to form, wherever Jesus makes an appearance both the scenario and the narrative change.

Jesus the creator of every living thing was about to display His authority and sovereignty. To fast forward the story, after Simon obeyed to let Jesus use his boat as a podium for preaching the gospel, his gloomy story changed for the better. Jesus entreated him to venture back into the waters despite it being daylight. He obeyed the instruction although from his vast fishing experience, daytime fishing was under ordinary circumstances untenable. The Bible says Simon managed to have a net breaking and boat sinking catch. This was a miracle by all accounts!

Jesus is a game changer. He changes dynamics, conventions and protocols. In the likely event that you are a person who suffers from business miscarriages, I want to introduce to you Jesus Christ of Nazareth. Make Him your partner in everything you do and success will be your portion. He finishes whatever He starts. Make Him the author and finisher of your faith.

You can shift and migrate from a life that is undersupplied in accomplishments and start on a new page and frequency with Jesus as your consultant. The choice is yours. When Jesus fills your senses, you become a success story. Everything you touch will have a touch of excellence. Jesus is the answer to every need. To God be the glory forevermore!

www.ingramcontent.com/pod-product-compliance
Lightning Source LLC
Chambersburg PA
CBHW021213160726
47994CB00001B/454